ENDORSEMENTS

Why should you read *I LIKE My Parents*? It is refreshingly honest. It is simple. It is practical. Any parent and even those who hope to be parents can find a starting point and make real headway immediately. Any parent. Even those who may be poster children for Dysfunctional Fathers and Mothers can get started today.

—John Anderson
President, Kingdom Congressional International

My friend Kevin and his wife Joyce have proven a stable and loving family is possible by holding to the principles of love, honor, and respect. The inclusion of young people sharing their own personal journeys authenticates the steps that are highlighted in this refreshing book. Truly this is a must-have book for today's parents interested in raising children that will be proud to declare "I like my parents."

—Rev. Paul Johansson, M.A.
President Emeritus, Elim Bible Institute and College
Chairman, New York School of Urban Ministry (NYSUM)

Kevin lays out the values we should instill in our children. I'm persuaded that, when we impart these values to their children, our homes will become havens of peace, tenderness, kindness, and warmth.

—**Bob Sorge**
Author, bobsorge.com

Teenage isolation and even outright rebellion against the family is growing rapidly worldwide. This book is a roadmap for anyone who wants to avoid and overcome these challenges for their own families.

—**Hon. Gregory W. Slayton**
Former US Ambassador to Bermuda
Founder of Family First Global
Author of *Be A Better Dad Today!*

Ronnie and I have become very close to Anna Joy, the Graves' oldest daughter, during her time in our city going to medical school. We have observed in her the rich qualities of love, honor, integrity, and a steadfast commitment to family and friends. She is a woman of true virtue and a testament to the success of the wisdom from the pages of this book put into action in a child's life. This book is a treasure of knowledge and a practical guide to raising exceptional adults!

—**Ronnie & Gayle Bennett**
(R) Executive Administrator, Church of the Highlands
(G) Accounting Team, Association of Related Churches

Kevin Graves, father of seven children, writes from a position of parenting coach after learning and applying many valuable lessons from his own outstanding parents. Graves models and recasts the vision for healthy parenting, and resets the bar to give hope and encouragement to parents and families everywhere. The book is easy to read and well worth the investment of time and money. Buy it, read it, put it into practice; then share it with others whom you really want to bless.

—**Dr. Bruce Cook**
Author, Speaker, Reformer, Chair of KCIAlliance.org

In *I LIKE My Parents!* you will hear the voices of real children who faced struggles and problems growing up and discovered the secrets of good parenting that will make them overcome and become successful in life.

Although I have known Kevin Graves for more than thirty years, while reading the manuscript I came to realize what a rich heritage Kevin has through his extended family in the United States, and the character-building principles communicated to him by his parents and grandparents, which he has built into the lives of his own children. I highly recommend this excellent book.

—**Dennis Balcombe**
Founder, Revival Christian Church, Hong Kong
Director, Revival Chinese Ministries International

In 1 Corinthians, the apostle Paul declared, "Be imitators of me." This book walks you through qualities—such as gratitude, honesty, smart decision making, and courageous disciplines—all with the purpose of raising children who learn to live and enjoy life that is a close reflection of their parents. This book is an enjoyable read as it challenges you with the truth that old is gold, while at the same time releases the young to run.

—**Pastor Chris Ball**
President of Elim Fellowship, USA

I LIKE My Parents!

The Art of Raising Awesome Kids

by Kevin A. Graves

Edited by Edie Mourey (furrowpress.com)

Cover design and photo on page 127 by Paul Rogers (paulrogersphotography.com)

Cover stock photo provided by Monkeybusinesimages/Pond5

Sheep, dog, and horse sketches on pages 7, 75, and 151, respectively, by Gretchen Finch (gretchenfinch.com)

Wildebeest painting on page 183 and painting of a child with her dog on the back cover by Nathan Graves

ISBN-13: 978-1986679596 (print edition)

DEDICATION

King Solomon penned these words three thousand years ago as if he knew my wife, Joyce:

> *She watches over the ways of her household,*
> *and does not eat the bread of idleness.*
> *Her children rise up and call her blessed,*
> *her husband also praises her:*
> *"Many daughters have done valiantly,*
> *but you surpass them all!"*[1]

All seven of my children adore their mother. She is dedicated, witty, diligent, and wise. Every day Joyce lives with purpose and effervescence. She has an endless flow of creativity. Most of the outstanding qualities we have fostered together in our children I learned from her.

This book is in honor of you, Joyce Graves, my bride of thirty-two years.

CONTENTS

ACKNOWLEDGMENTS

I feel a bit like my eldest daughter, her husband (with our two granddaughters in tow), and our third daughter in the pictures they've sent through our family chat this past week. They stood at the base of the vast mountain range at Zion National Park with towering peaks serving as a breathtaking backdrop. Two days later, they were perched on those same peaks, sending us pics of the luscious valleys below.

As I look down on this completed volume, I realize that I never could have climbed this mountain alone. In many ways this was as it should be, a family venture. Joyce brought numerous useful suggestions and feedback. Anna gave recommendations on the book cover and other finishing touches. Nathan contributed his wildebeest painting and the painting of the child with her dog on the back cover. Liz, Tabitha, and Jeremy all contributed valuable stories to three of the chapters. Daniel and Charlotte had to sacrifice some daddy time as I honed in to pull the book together. My deepest thanks to you all!

Each chapter has a child's contribution. Besides my three children's stories, my heartfelt thanks go out to: (Singapore) Shania Chen, Natalie Chan, and Rachel Yang; (Philippines) Francine and Rachel Yu; (Indonesia) Daniel and Jennifer Hadirahardja; (Malaysia) Jeh Sie Tan; and (U.S.) Meredith Scott. Your testimonies are going to help young people in many nations to be honest and courageous like you were when you wrote your stories. A thousand thanks to each of you!

Deepest thanks to Edie Mourey for your edits, suggestions, and words of encouragement. You went above and beyond the call of duty. And thanks to you, Paul Rogers, for your photos and your splendid work on the cover design.

I cannot imagine better sheep, dog, and horse sketches than those provided by our friend of many years, Gretchen Finch. You have loved them all in your life, and now we get to love them, too, through your gift.

Thanks to all our dear friends from Family First Global, who have been an example and inspiration to Joyce and me in many more ways than the writing of *I LIKE My Parents!*

Finally, thanks to my mom and dad, whose example and single-minded dedication to my brothers and our families, if written, would need its own section in the library. And last, and most certainly not least, thank You, God.

FOREWORD

I have celebrity parents. When they got married in December of 1956, their marriage made it to the front page of the national newspapers. The reason for that is my dad was a cripple. He contracted arthritis when he was eighteen, and five surgeries later, he was consigned to walk with a pair of crutches for the rest of his life. When he was dating my mom, he kept on saying to her that he did not want her to pity him. Each time he would try to talk her out of the marriage, she would love him even more.

My dad was a bit of a recluse. I remember he would come back from work, go to his study, shut the door, and listen to his classical music. I never really got to know him. And because of his condition, my brothers and I couldn't do things normal kids did, like run around in the garden, play ball, or swim. My dad died of a heart attack when he was fifty, and it crushed me. His death left a void in my heart.

My mom was the real strength in the family. She became a model to us. When she was born again and became an on-fire Christian, I remember vividly how much I wanted what she had! She was kind, gentle, and patient—truly a great mom. She took care of me and my two brothers singlehandedly after my dad died. She saw us through our growing-up years, painful as it was, then all the way through university. We owe so much to her.

In 1 Timothy 5:8 Paul says, "But if anyone does not provide for his own, and especially for those of his household, he has denied the faith and is worse than an unbeliever." Paul doesn't mince his words here. Looking after our own and caring for our families, especially our aged parents, is one of the fundamental characteristics of the Christian faith.

Yeah, so I *like* my parents. No, they weren't perfect. We all have inconsistencies and imperfections. I don't know if I have been a good father. God knows I try hard. But my kids will be the judge of that. I think that even the best parents have made painful mistakes. But if there is one couple who in my eyes have been "celebrity parents," a couple whom I have admired for years, it is Kevin and Joyce Graves. They have been a true example for us here in the church. They have raised amazing children, and as you will discover through the pages of this book, they are a godly example of how parenting should be done. Kevin and Joyce are the real deal, and I have so much to learn from them.

Ultimately, our children are our legacy. *I LIKE My Parents!* will help ensure you leave a lasting legacy.

Rev. Yang Tuck Yoong
Senior Pastor
Cornerstone Community Church

Chapter One

INTRODUCTION

*R*elationships are a two-way street. For example, if I want to have a good friend, I need to be a good friend. I need to give myself to the friendship. Similarly, if I want to have a good marriage, I must invest in it. I cannot demand that my wife be loyal and honest and caring when I don't give her any quality time or communicate with her about my plans or remember our anniversary. If we had entered marriage thinking, *Well, I'll give 50 percent if you'll give 50 percent,* that would have been a disaster! We must give our all to each other and the relationship, and that means *both* of us giving 100 percent.

The parent/child relationship is another relationship requiring mutual participation and cooperation. It demands deep commitment, sacrifice, patience, grace, and skill. It is the longest human relationship most of us will ever have, unless we happen to be married for fifty years or more to a certain person. If the parent/child relationship is pleasant, it can bring us some of the greatest joys we'll ever know. If it is painful, we can suffer emotional, psychological, and even physical effects over our lifetimes.

My wife and I have raised seven amazing children. I know that does not necessarily qualify me to write about parenting, but at the very least it has given me many opportunities to learn from my mistakes! Sometimes, I've wondered who is raising whom.

I do bring a couple of distinct advantages to parenthood, however. First, I have wonderful parents. They have modeled sacrifice, commitment, dedication, selflessness, and support to me in more ways than I can count. I am so grateful for them.

Second, I was determined to get this parenting thing right. Actually, I should say *we* were determined. My wife, Joyce, has earned my praise and the respect of scores of people over the years who have watched her distill her motherly duties with the right balance of affection and skill. Together, we have sought to put our family first—above careers, ambitions, or any other relationships. We've taken courses and attended seminars, and I've done a LOT of reading on the subject of how to be a better dad. We are throwing in our all, our 100 percent!

As I've read parenting books, I've made a discovery. Most books talk about how to be good parents rather than how to raise good kids. There is an important difference. In other words, there are numerous books out there on *parent*-ing but not a lot on *kid*-ing. Sons and daughter are not, after all, passive participants in this process. Our goal is to produce something dynamic, principled, and eternal in *them*. If, for instance, the emphasis is on what *we* need to do to discipline our children, we miss the point if the discipline does not result in positive and substantive changes in them. This is true in every facet of our parenting journey. I will consider myself to have hit the target if my children are giving 100 percent, too. That's the two-way-street part of relationships.

With this in mind, I embarked on the journey of writing a book that identifies twelve characteristics of healthy, positive, and secure children. Children with these qualities are not spectators in the home, rather they are active contributors.

The emphasis here is on what they are becoming. If I focus on what I do as a parent, I may produce the desired *behavior* in my son or daughter yet not see heart transformation. The point is not action but essence. It answers the question not only of what our children should do, but why and as whom. We move towards spontaneous, and not robotic, responses—that which springs from inside and has become natural, organic, or second nature. We don't merely teach our children responsibility; we help them become responsible. We don't just teach them to save money; we show them how to become generous. There is even a subtle yet critical difference between teaching them not to lie and encouraging them to become honest. Our goal should not only be that our children respect us, but that they enjoy being around us as well.

A NOTE TO SINGLE PARENTS

There are no perfect or ideal families. If you are a single parent, or are bearing the load of raising your children without the full support or cooperation of your spouse, I want to offer you a word of hope. You can do it. You can raise awesome kids even if you have to do it alone. You can nurture the twelve qualities that are in this book. Insist that your children are honest. Guide them in choosing great friends. Don't accept the fallacy that they have to rebel, or that they cannot stand up to peer pressure.

Many amazing people have been raised by single parents. Debbie Phelps does not have a single gold medal around her neck, but as a single mom she set out to overcome every obstacle and make her son into a winner. Eighteen Olympic gold medals later, Michael Phelps praises his mom for giving him the guts and courage to literally leave all rivals in his wake.

When Michael was young and a teacher spoke disparagingly about him, that he would never be able to keep up with other kids, his mother became determined to prove the teacher wrong that Michael could not become an extraordinary child. She dug in: "I knew that, if I collaborated with Michael, he could achieve anything he set his mind to."[2] She was right. And if medals were given out to parents who exhibit this can-do mindset, she should have a place on the top podium.

With determination and commitment, you can raise winners, too. Like Debbie, dig in.

AN OVERVIEW

My hope is that *I LIKE My Parents!* will facilitate times of your working together with your kids. Each chapter has a child's contribution (which you can even read together), and some suggestions of things that you can do together to nurture that chapter's particular characteristic. Three of the contributions are from my own children. The other contributors are kids from five different nations, ranging in age from five years old to early adulthood. Their message? Having these qualities has made a difference in their lives.

We live in an age of information overload. We don't need more theories; we need tools that really work. With that in mind, I've created "Put It To Work" guides at the end of each chapter to help you engage your children in discussions about these qualities. The more you engage your children in discussions and put these qualities to work, the more you are helping them to acquire the qualities—the more you're helping them to become.

I have also organized the chapters conveniently into three sections. Each section is represented by a different animal. This is both for ease of understanding, as well as to offer another discussion point to bridge to your kids. The sections are:

- **Sheep Qualities:** Sheep are best known for their manner. Quiet, cute, and cuddly, sheep are unperturbed by the world around them. They manage to keep a good *attitude* through the ups and downs of life.

- **Dog Qualities:** Dogs are best known for their undying loyalty. "Man's best friend" is the most relational of all God's creatures, a good reminder to us that, at the end of the day, what we value most is each other.

- **Horse Qualities:** Horses are powerful and

majestic. But in order for horses to be enjoyed, they have to be tamed and then trained to reach their full potentials.

The Old Testament ends in dramatic fashion with the words that God will "turn the hearts of the parents to the children, and the hearts of the children to their parents" (Malachi 4:6 NIV). Whereas books and conferences address the issue of parents turning their hearts to their children (and rightfully so!), this book explores what it looks like when a child's heart turns back to his or her mom and dad. It asks, how do parents nurture this kind of response from their children? What can children do to plant themselves in the soil of a healthy family? At a time when families around the world are facing tremendous pressures, what can be done to make children say, "I LIKE my parents!"?

Part One

SHEEP QUALITIES

Sheep are best known for their manner. Quiet, cute, and cuddly, sheep are unperturbed by the world around them. They manage to keep a good *attitude* through the ups and downs of life. In this section, we will explore the following sheep-like qualities which we hope our children will embrace: gratitude, honesty, obedience, and honor.

Chapter Two

AN ATTITUDE OF GRATITUDE

Gratitude is the healthiest of all human emotions. The more you express gratitude for what you have, the more likely you will have even more to express gratitude for.[3]

— ZIG ZIGLAR

*W*eekends can get really busy around our house. Sometimes, it feels as though we are all going in different directions. But the other day, we planned to have a leisurely brunch and then just spend some family time together. After singing a couple of songs, I asked everyone to share something for which they were grateful. It started slowly at first, but then the interaction picked up as my children began sharing their gratitude for various things. Charles Dickens wrote: "Reflect upon your present blessings, of which every man has plenty; not on your past misfortunes, of which all men have some."[4]

The world "out there" can often hit you like a lead pillow, a barrage of negativity coming at you from every direction—from the news, or complaints, or verbal attacks. One of the most healthy habits we can nurture is to frequently and sincerely count our blessings. Then, once we have counted them, we shouldn't keep them to ourselves. *A blessing shared is a dark cloud spared.*

SUNNY WEATHER

Twenty-first-century man may not have figured out how to control the weather, but gratitude is one thing that is guaranteed to change atmospheric conditions in relationships. *Thanks* is a powerful word! With it you can stop a relational storm that is forming, prevent eruptions, and break a cold snap. When I show appreciation, I bless the person to whom I have spoken. I draw him or her closer to me, and I nurture my own heart in the process. Today, if I acknowledge an accomplishment, or express to others that something has been done well or someone has been helpful, I am sowing good seeds into my relationships. These sown seeds will produce a harvest of good fruit tomorrow.

Wise parents find a way to harness the gift of thanksgiving to create a positive atmosphere in the home. Wise children find ways to contribute to the atmospheric conditions of their home, helping the home become a place where everyone feels sheltered from the blizzards that judgment, comparisons, nitpicking, whining, or nagging create. While we hope to influence the environments where we go to school, work, or play, the home is the one place where the winds and waves should obey us, where we are not subject to high pressure, high tides, or tempests. There has to be a determination, with everyone playing his or her part, that in our home the "weather" is under our control—that when we rise each day the forecast reads, "Sunny and clear!"

SAY SOMETHING NICE

When we fail to nurture an attitude of gratitude, we tend to take things, or other people, for granted. Think about it. It is very hard to be thankful *and* disappointed at the same time. A mom can plan meals for a week, carefully form a budget and put a list together for shopping, and then go out and buy the things needed to make healthy meals for the family. Even without slicing the first onion or marinating the meat, she has already worked for something that many never give a second thought. By the time she has completed the meal, set the table, fed the family, and cleaned up after everyone, a whole lot of loving has gone into each and every step involved in evening dinner. When children quickly sit down, wolf down their food, and then rush on to their next "important" activity, all without stopping to consider these things, much less saying thanks, something precious and necessary has been violated.

Even if Mom is not doing it for thanks, that does not make it right to say nothing. On the other hand, when children (and Dad) tell her they appreciate the thoughtful and tireless effort, these words put wind in her sails. Or better yet, if they offer her help in any or all of the meal prep and cleanup, she feels appreciated. Rather than feeling like she is peddling uphill all day long, our praise and help suddenly propel her over the crest of the mountain. Knowing that the hard work of the climb has been noticed, she can effortlessly coast down the other side, contented while taking in the views. Her gift to us has turned into our gift to her, as it ought to be.

Charlotte is the youngest of our children, and she has been blessed with the most wonderful disposition. She is content, and cheerful, and enjoys her family and her life very much. She also has a gift which she wields as a powerful tool to tickle and inspire: She loves to write notes of encouragement. Sometimes, they are in the form of a card with adorable drawings, stickers, or stamps. It's too precious. I have often thought how nice it would be if every home could have a Charlotte!

Jennifer from Indonesia was seven when she discovered that being thankful is a great way to spread happiness to others.

———

I have noticed a habit that my dad and mom have. Every time a waiter or waitress delivers our order, or any time our nanny or I give them things that they have asked for, they will always say, "terima kasih," which means *thank you* in Bahasa Indonesian. At first I was surprised. I thought to myself, *Why are they thanking me? If they ask me to get something for them, it's only natural to do what they have asked of me.* Then one day, I got up the courage to ask my dad about it.

"Dad . . . why do you always say *thank you* every time somebody gives you something or does what you have asked them to do?"

With a smile, he said, "Well, we should show our

appreciation for the time, energy, and effort that someone has made for us. Everyone is entitled to this basic courtesy. Besides, when I or Mom ask somebody else to help us, we interrupt their activities, and then they sacrifice of their own time to help us. So we have to appreciate it. That's why we say *thank you*. We also would do the same for you, my princess. So remember, whenever somebody has helped you or has given you something, no matter how 'small' or 'simple' it may seem, never forget to say *thank you*. That's our family value!"

Since then, every time somebody gives me something, or somebody helps me to get something that I ask for, I too follow up with a *thank you*. It's simple, but seeing a big smile on the people to whom I say it. Well, it's a priceless blessing to me. I'm sure grateful my dad and mom have taught me such a valuable lesson.

———

Jennifer's dad says that, five years later, she's still a very positive person. It goes to show you: A thankful person is a happy person.

GRATITUDE IS A CHOICE

When I choose to be grateful, I am choosing to see the glass half full rather than half empty. It means I am focusing on the positive things in a person, or a situation, rather than the negative. I am repelling darkness and inviting light into my friendships. I am offering hope rather than giving place to despair. I am seeing progress being made rather than magnifying imperfections.

We don't buy a lollipop and lick the stick. We go for the sweet stuff! Such is the power of a grateful heart. It is able to celebrate how far we've come rather than bemoan the fact that we still have a long ways to go. Gratitude acknowledges the good in others so that we are more naturally patient towards the areas of their lives that are still a work in progress. What kind of person do you like to be around? A grumbler or a singer? A faultfinder or an exhorter? Who do you want to represent you? A prosecuting attorney or a defense lawyer?!

I don't mean to suggest that we ignore those blind spots, weaknesses, or foibles with which our friends or family members struggle. But it does mean that the attitude we have when pointing out these things to them has to be bathed in grace. Rightness is often not judged by content but by countenance, not by terminology but by tone. One of the valuable lessons I have learned from Joyce is teaching our children that whatever they say or do must be done with the right attitude of heart. To reward another person for doing something with the wrong attitude is another way of saying it is acceptable to pay lip-service or the attitude of the heart doesn't really matter. Is this the message that we want to pass on to our children—that being fake is acceptable? I don't think so.

MAKING DEPOSITS

When I frequently express my gratitude for another, and point out the ways which he or she has benefitted or blessed me, it is like making deposits into his or her emotional bank account. Then when there is a need to remind, or correct, even rebuke another, these "savings" can be withdrawn. The other person hears and receives these words without them causing offense or hurt because I have invested in the positive things which build confidence and trust. In his best-selling book, *Be A Better Dad Today*, Professor Gregory W. Slayton puts it this way:

> Too many parenting books today talk about "building Johnny's self-esteem" based on false praise and empty words. When our son gets a C on a math test because he didn't study, he doesn't need to hear how smart he is and what a great student he is, or what a lousy teacher he has, or other excuses. He needs to hear that he must study harder the next time. But when he gets an A (or, for some students, a B+) on a test because he studied hard and prepared well, he needs to hear how truly proud we are of him. Ten parts love and praise for every one part discipline is a pretty good balance.[5]

The same principle applies for the ways sons and daughters speak to their parents. Kids should acknowledge or praise their parents for making an extra effort or a sacrifice, or for helping to put on a great birthday party for them. Why would we think this should be a one-way street? When children discover the joy of thanking and praising their parents, they will wonder why they were not doing this before.

We all contribute to the kind of household we live in. Changing the "culture" in the family begins with each of us.

BLESSED ARE THE POOH IN HEART

A. A. Milne has done all of us a great service in giving us Winnie the Pooh and friends. They may be a bunch of imaginary stuffed animals come to life, but each one has an endearing and unforgettable disposition that keeps young and old coming back to them. Who could ever forget the pure-heartedness of that "silly old bear"? Or what about Eeyore, the somewhat forlorn donkey who never gets his tail on right? And how about lovable Piglet? We all need some Piglets in our lives to remind us that every cloud has a silver lining. The secret to his magnetism? Milne put it this way: "Piglet noticed that even though he had a Very Small Heart, it could hold a rather large amount of Gratitude."[6]

Unfortunately, there are some very aggressive media and social trends that work directly against attempts to raise a grateful and positive generation. Our children are not choosing between Eeyore and Piglet. Consider the most watched video online in a twenty-four-hour period when it was released in 2013, "Wrecking Ball." What does a naked singer perched upon a wrecking ball say about the values of youth culture today? How many rappers have platinum albums that record songs about being thankful for living in the most prosperous generation in history?

As parents, we have to realize that a flood of negative passions has been released and directed towards the younger generation. Our youth have to guard their hearts from the kinds of influence that breed an attitude of defiance rather than of gratitude. Parents can put up safeguards, and even be vigilant, but it is like saying someone will not get wet in a downpour. A good umbrella will help, but only the naïve believes that something is not going to get wet. Are we sending our children out in the worst of thunderstorms? What kind of an umbrella have you provided them with when the monsoons do come?

PROFESSIONAL MOURNERS

The same could be said of mainstream media as well. Bill O'Reilly, once the most watched news commentator in America, said the "Grievance Industry" has become a multi-billion dollar bust for people who incite the basest nature of man with propaganda about rare occurrences or fringe news items. Their goal? To stir up ugly sentiments and provoke anger or disappointment in people in order to prey upon their attention and even present themselves as special advocates, spokespersons, or "saviors" for so-called forgotten causes or injustices. One sour grape in a bunch is interpreted by these opportunists as a bunch of sour grapes.

We unsuspecting people do not realize that, once these hucksters have convinced us the grapes are bad, they are ready to sell us *their* fruit at a one-time, just-for-us price! I cannot imagine making a living agitating people into believing they are victims, or deprived, or being taken advantage of. Wouldn't it be better to remind people of the strides that are being made or to encourage them to be content with what they have?

Positive news doesn't usually make the headlines; in fact, sometimes it doesn't even make the back page! There's no money to be made off "good news" in the smorgasbord of twenty-first-century news outlets.

Apparently, these media-types are not new. Many

cultures have had their professional mourners and criers for thousands of years, even to the present day. These discovered they could make good money singing their dirges, so they kept singing the song of the dead among the living. African-American leader and advisor to presidents, Booker T. Washington, observed more than one hundred years ago (1911):

> There is a class of colored people who make a business of keeping the troubles, the wrongs, and the hardships of the Negro race before the public. Some of these people do not want the Negro to lose his grievances, because they do not want to lose their jobs. There is a certain class of race-problem solvers who don't want the patient to get well.[7]

Though his words cut across the social justice outcries of our day, nonetheless, he pointed to those he thought continued to stir strife.

IMMUNIZING AGAINST BAD ATTITUDES

The existence of this hidden and dark force which is at work quietly poisoning the waters of our lives and cultures demands a response. First of all, we should acknowledge that this bent is in the heart of us all. Salacious tales and illicit stories can be seducing, even intoxicating. We cannot just assume that the tentacles of such narratives will not reach an unsuspecting friend or loved one. To do nothing is like leaving a pile of food out in the open. First come the "harmless" ants, then the cockroaches, and then the rats. So what can we do to build up our family defenses? Are there any "weapons" which can be used to drive these forces back?

Here are some suggestions:

- **Give thanks among yourselves.** Don't take the things your family members do for you for granted. Remind one another to be grateful, and remember the words of William Arthur Ward: "Feeling gratitude and not expressing it is like wrapping a present and not giving it."[8] We would not do that for each other on birthdays; neither should we *forget* to unwrap our thanks.

- **Have a "No Criticism" rule.** Don't let destructive and demeaning talk about another family member be uttered. Hold each other to account in this so that you create a wall around your home to keep out negativity. When correction or instruction is needed, it should be done redemptively so as to help your child see a better way of relating.

- **Set aside some specific times or ways to show your appreciation.** An example of this is our family Christmas stocking tradition. Besides small trinkets and gifts, we all take the time to write notes of blessing and encouragement to all the people in the household. We place the notes in each others' stockings. Sharing these little notes has become the most anticipated part of our Christmas celebration.

- **Monitor your own and each other's GIGO quotient.** GIGO stands for *Garbage In, Garbage Out,* and was especially popular in the early days of computer science. It refers to the fact that computers can only produce by logical processes, meaning if the wrong data is inputed, then wrong data will be outputted. Within the family, build a transparent value system that says, "Since I don't want garbage to come out of me, help me to make sure I am not putting garbage in." Be transparent and hold each other to account lest the garbage begins to pile up. Left unchecked, it will start to stink and attract unwelcome "visitors" to everyone's chagrin.

- **Tell the stories of noble and exemplary people.** Positive stories can be challenging to find, but there are still some feel-good movies out there, or books that have wholesome content and encourage the kind of value systems we want to see exhibited in our homes. We are greatly mistaken if we think that books about "nice people" have to be boring.

Below is an excerpt from a great book, *The Hiding Place,* which I read to my eight-, eleven-, and thirteen-year-olds each night before going to bed. The excerpt is of a conversation that took place while two sisters were in a concentration camp in WWII Germany for being a part of an underground movement that rescued hundreds of Jews from potential extermination:

"That's it, Corrie! That's His answer. 'Give thanks in all circumstances!' That's what we can do. We can start right now to thank God for every single thing about this new barracks!

I stared at her, then around me at the dark, foul-aired room.

"Such as?" I said.

"Such as being assigned here together."

I bit my lip. "Oh yes, Lord Jesus!"

"Such as what you're holding in your hands."

I looked down at the Bible. "Yes! Thank you, dear Lord, that there was no inspection when we entered here! Thank you for all these women, here in this room, who will meet You in these pages."[9]

Author Corrie Ten Boom went on to become an internationally well-known symbol of courage and conviction after surviving the most horrific conditions imaginable under Hitler's brutal regime. Despite the deplorable surroundings, she painted a portrait of her sister, Betsie, as completely contented throughout. When Betsie died after nearly a year in these squalid prison camps, the presiding nurse was standing over her corpse in awe when Corrie walked into the room and saw the radiant face of her fifty-nine-year-old sister who miraculously lay as if sleeping, her countenance renewed to its youthfulness.

Gratitude is always the right attitude. One of our favorite movies is the 1997 Italian film *Life is Beautiful*. Also written against the backdrop of a Nazi concentration camp, the star, a Jewish bookshop owner by the name of Guido, artfully employed humor and fun to shield his son, Guisue, from the horrors of the camp by pretending it was all a complex game for which one could gain points and win prizes for good behavior and making wise choices. Like Betsie, Guido manages to paste smilie stickers on a world full of cruelty and injustice. While none of us lives in a perfect world, that some can live in such an imperfect one and yet turn it into a place of cheer is one of the grandest lessons of all that we can learn and pass on to our loved ones.

Whatever it takes to cultivate a grateful disposition in your life, in your home, and among the people with whom you are in contact day in and day out, consider it worth every ounce of effort. I have also observed those who have never discovered "Life is Beautiful," who have never known the wonder of a life lived in the grace of a thankful heart. Harboring pessimism, backbiting, and criticism, their path is lined with bitter herbs and thorns, and becomes more and more unpleasant as they reach the end of their life's journey. How much better to have lived . . . like Guido, or Betsie, or Piglet.

PUT IT TO WORK

- This chapter began with our family sitting around after a leisurely lunch and **asking everyone to share something for which they are grateful.** Look for the opportunity to try it! For some, this could be a spontaneous and natural exercise. Another way to do this is to pass everyone a piece of paper and ask them to put two things down for which they are grateful, then share in turn. The main thing is to choose your moment wisely, when parents and children alike are relaxed and not in response to a tense encounter.

- Put a "No Criticism Zone" sign on the door of your house for a while and see what happens!

- Read the section together from *The Hiding Place* and Betsie's "attitude of gratitude" in this chapter. Ask the family how they feel they can make an adjustment to become more "Betsie-like."

- Try leaving a personal note of blessing or encouragement inside Christmas stockings.

- Rent *Life is Beautiful* and watch it together. You'll be glad you did!

Chapter Three

BE HONEST

Honesty is the first chapter in the book of wisdom. [10]

— THOMAS JEFFERSON

$\mathcal{I}$ will never forget what my cultural anthropology teacher said about the day his life "was changed forever." He had been living in a foreign land where he was highly respected and his expertise was well sought after. Life abroad had plateaued for him, and he had nearly given up hope of having any meaningful friendships with the local population.

Then one day, when faced with some real struggles, he humbled himself and asked the local people for help. Completely absent of any pretense, and no longer hiding under the cloak of being the "expert," he honestly told them, "Look, I am really in need here!"

Suddenly, the whole atmosphere changed. The people

became warm and cordial to him like never before. The pedestal upon which he had stood, out of touch and unreal, was lowered, and he stood before them face to face, eye to eye, and heart to heart. That day was the first day of what became a lasting friendship, whereby the local people took my teacher into their hearts and culture as though he were a native son. He has enjoyed this relationship with them for the past fifty years.

BECOMING TRANS-PARENTS

When it comes to parenting, "Honesty is the best policy." Although there is no place where we should feel as free to be who we really are than among our family, even within our own homes, we still may put on masks and airs, or protect and primp an image of ourselves. Although honesty should begin with us as parents, as was the case with my professor, we parents don't always put on an honest face. Maybe we think our children should also see us standing high on a pedestal. Maybe we think that our distance will help to prop up our status, causing our children to give us the respect we deserve. Maybe we think that, if they know we have weaknesses, or struggles, they will shun, judge, or shy away from us.

Recently, I had one of those raw, candid moments with my thirteen-year-old son. I told him about some of the battles I went through when I was a teenager. I told him that I went through a period when I was more concerned about what my peers thought about me than I should have been. I confessed that I ended up doing some things which really were not "me," just so I could gain the approval of so-called *friends*. I told him that I took some risks I wished I had not taken. I told him how my foolishness had landed me in trouble. I told him I had regrets.

My son's response was immediate and tender. He saw me as real and approachable. He saw me as someone who might understand some of the things that he was facing. He also saw me as someone who had survived the turmoils of youth to become successful as an adult, which I suspect helped him to see that he, too, could be successful one day. He opened up to me. Now that he could relate to me, he wanted me to be a part of his struggles rather than to try hiding them from me.

Because I was honest, my son dared to be honest, too. If I have given him the gift of being honest in life, I may have given him one of the most important keys to becoming a contented and successful person over a lifetime. Then, hopefully, one day when the time is right, he will have this conversation with his own sons and daughters.

"CONDEMNED"

No healthy relationship can exist without honesty. Honesty opens the door to trust, and without trust the foundation of our relationships is shaken and under the threat of collapsing.

I've had the opportunity to help with relief efforts following disasters ranging from flooding to large-scale earthquakes. When I was a young man, I volunteered to do cleanup after a major flood had ravaged our city business center. I remember being surprised by what I saw after the waters had receded. Some of the affected homes and businesses were marked for demolition. Although they looked solid to the naked, inexperienced eye, dangerous cracks had formed in the foundations of these buildings, making them uninhabitable as they were hazardous to live in. I remember seeing a red sign on these buildings with a familiar word on it, but I had only known the definition of the word in another context: *condemned*. To me the word described a person who had been convicted of a crime, one who had been found guilty of breaking the law. It was then that I learned of another definition:

A condemned building is in such bad condition that it is not safe to live in, and so its owners are officially ordered to pull it down or repair it.

Relationships that lack *transparency*—where there is a hiding of facts, bending of truth, moving on to increasing deceit and cover-up—are in danger of the *condemned* sign being nailed conspicuously to them. It is imperative to conduct a thorough inspection of the "structural integrity" of these relationships before the condition is so bad that they are "no longer safe to live in."

I had a similar revelation working with an international team doing relief after a major earthquake in China. In this case, some buildings had completely collapsed following the big quake itself. Though many buildings remained standing, the people lived in tents in open spaces away from the buildings, because there was no way to tell the extent of the damage to the structures without a thorough inspection by professionals. If neighboring homes were destroyed, it was likely that these homes had suffered irreparable damage to their foundations. In such cases, even the subsequent, much weaker tremors could send a seemingly fine home crashing to the ground.

Damage caused by dishonesty over time is like this. It might not necessarily be the big incident that causes the house to collapse if the foundations have been compromised. If the conditions are ripe, even a tremor may be enough to raze what has taken years to build.

If we want our homes to be a haven of security for every member, we owe it to each other to shun lies and deception, in any form, and to cultivate honesty.

I have taken the time to describe the condemned home to illustrate the extreme importance of honesty among family members. Indeed, the security of your home will be threatened in a dishonest environment. If we lie to those among whom there should be no pretense or nothing hidden, then what will become of us when we engage the world outside the confines of our homes that is already corrupted and anesthetized by persistent exposure to half-truths and duplicity?

THE TALE OF TWO PRESIDENTS

I want each of my children to have a positive impact on the world around them. Honored and respected leaders and people who have the deepest influence on their surroundings understand the importance of integrity in securing the confidence of others. When trust erodes, so does a leader's ability to dictate, direct, and advise.

The most famous story of the first American President, George Washington, which has been passed down generation to generation, reinforces our idolization of a man who earned our nation's respect. It is about an honest deed he did when he was a child. In this tale, he proved he had the courage to tell the truth no matter what it would cost him:

When George was about six years old, he was made the wealthy master of a hatchet of which, like most little boys, he was extremely fond. He went about chopping everything that came his way. One day, as he wandered about the garden amusing himself by hacking his mother's pea sticks, he found a beautiful, young English cherry tree, of which his father was most proud. He tried the edge of his hatchet on the trunk of the tree and barked it so that it died.

Some time after this, his father discovered what had happened to his favorite tree. He came into the house in great anger, and demanded to know who the mischievous person was who had cut away the bark. Nobody could tell him anything about it. Just then George, with his little hatchet, came into the room. "George," said his father, "do you know who has killed my beautiful little cherry tree yonder in the garden? I would not have taken five guineas for it!"

This was a hard question to answer, and for a moment George was staggered by it, but quickly recovering himself he cried: *"I cannot tell a lie, father, you know I cannot tell a lie!* I did cut it with my little hatchet." The anger died out of his father's face, and taking the boy tenderly in his arms, he said: "My son, that you should not be afraid, to tell the truth is more to me than a thousand trees! Yes—though they were blossomed with silver and had leaves of the purest gold!"[11]

The most revered and celebrated of all American Presidents is Abraham Lincoln. Again, the character of integrity cultivated from childhood stands out as being the most striking and endearing portrait of this demure leader:

As a young man, Abraham Lincoln worked as a general store clerk. One evening he was counting the money in the drawers after closing and found that he was a few cents over what should have been in the drawer. When he realized that he had accidentally short-changed a customer earlier that day, Lincoln walked a long distance to return the money to the customer.

On another occasion Lincoln discovered that he had given a woman too little tea for her money. He put what he owed her in a package and personally delivered it to the woman—who never realized that she was not given the proper amount of tea until Lincoln showed up at her doorstep![12]

Lincoln's integrity and insistence on honesty became even more apparent in his law practice. In his book, *An Honest Calling: The Law Practice of Abraham Lincoln,* Mark Steiner notes that:

A relative by marriage, Augustus H. Chapman, recalled: "In his law practice on the Wabash Circuit he was noted for unswerving honesty. People learned to love him ardently, devotedly, and juries listened intently, earnestly, receptively to the sad-faced, earnest man. I remember one case which revealed his honest trait of character. It was a case in which he was for the defendant. Satisfied of his client's innocence, it depended mainly on one witness. That witness told on the stand under oath what Abe knew to be a lie, and no one else knew. When he arose to plead the case, he said: "Gentlemen, I depended on this witness to clear my client. He has lied. I ask that no attention be paid to his testimony. Let his words be stricken out, if my case fails. I do not wish to win in this way."

Lincoln carried his regard for the truth through his years at the White House. He, himself, was forthright and deeply sincere. It seems as if some of his colleagues wondered if he could ever tell a lie. During the Civil War, President Lincoln stated, *"I ain't been caught lying yet, and I don't mean to be."* For Lincoln, the truth was not worth sacrificing for any gain, no matter how large that gain may have been.

Lincoln didn't need to lie to save the Union, to unite the people, and free slaves, and lead a nation. Perhaps that is why he remains a hero to so many around the world, and an inspiration to leaders well into the future. From his work as a clerk to his duties as a president, Lincoln's honesty was unwavering, showing that telling the truth is an essential lesson for all, no matter who you are or what you do.[13]

The history of the world is a record of the risings and fallings of kings and generals, tycoons and great thinkers. Many were powerful but also tyrannical, manipulative, machiavellian. Among those who are held in highest esteem by successive generations and are adored with our hearts and not just our heads are ones whose gifts and abilities were painted with strokes of honesty, sincerity, and truthfulness. The stories of Presidents Washington and Lincoln underscore that these qualities were instilled into their lives from the time they were young.

THE BEST POLICY

Honesty is something Joyce and I have always strictly required of our children. Whenever we doubt the accuracy of what our child says, no matter how small or seemingly insignificant, we make it a point to correct immediately, applying discipline when we feel it necessary.

As there is no "safe" fire in the forest, there is no innocuous lie. All raging forest fires begin with a small flame. If you don't face the fire when it is small, when it grows out of control, lives and property are put in harm's way. It is the same with lying. It is not safe in any form. Once a habit of covering up faults or embellishing facts has formed, it's like the proverbial genie that has gotten out of the bottle, unwilling or unable to return to the cramped space from which it has escaped. A ten-year-old boy from Asia learned this important lesson early in life. The "best policy" should serve him well for decades!

———

One day I got a really bad grade on my test. Although it

was "just" in Mandarin, and I don't really like the subject, but still, failing was very, very bad.

At first I thought I would just keep it to myself because I was afraid to tell my parents about it. They seldom ask questions about my test grades, because they trust me enough. But then I remembered my dad was always teaching us about honesty. He would say something like, "Once people find out you're lying, it will be hard for people to trust you again. And trust is essential in this world. So don't ever lie to us. No matter how bad the situation, whether it's on your grades, or a mistake that you've made, always tell us the truth. Yes we will scold you, and punish you if needed, but we'll still love you, and appreciate your honesty."

So that afternoon, when my dad got home, I decided to tell him the truth. "Dad, I just got my Mandarin test result back . . . And . . . I failed!"

I was so ready to hear him scold me, but instead he smiled! Then he said: "Well, Daniel . . . I appreciate your honesty . . . Thank you for that . . . And now, let's talk about failing your Mandarin test."

To make a long story short, my parents registered me to join a Mandarin course. And since that time, I have never ever failed a Mandarin test again.

I am grateful that my parents taught me about the importance of honesty. By being truthful, not only did I gain and maintain their trust, but the problems I was having with my Chinese studies also were solved. Indeed, it pays to be honest!

———

We have all heard one of Aesop's Fables titled "The Boy Who Cried Wolf." The first time he cried out for help, the whole village in this sheep-herding village was mobilized to drive the imaginary wolf from ravaging their flocks. The second time he cried, it was the same. But dishonesty has a way of catching up with us, so when the boy cried wolf the third time and there truly *was* a wolf attacking the unsuspecting sheep, the villagers all stayed home. Innocent sheep were slaughtered on the hillsides of the town that day. The moral of the story is clear: If we sow deception, we will reap disaster sooner or later.

WHITE LIES?

Somewhere in time, the concept of a "white lie"—a slight *bending* of the truth, a minor distortion of details—evolved. It is given special status by virtue of its perceived pettiness. It sounds incredible, but many deem it a socially permissible falsehood. But beware. Armed with this seemingly harmless tool, the twelve-inch fish that was caught grows to fifteen, eighteen, or twenty inches as the fisherman's story is told amid the oohs and awes of chorusing approval! White lies, like the fish, only tend to grow bigger with time. This is the nature of a lie, whether its white, green, or incandescent!

If we allow our children to develop a casual attitude towards what is true, we will have done them a great disservice. They may get hired for a job and think it's "no big deal" to overstate something because it has been etched into their minds that a little lie goes without consequence.

When a child grows up and loses a job, or violates relationships because of a habitual pattern of misrepresenting truth, he or she will have to live with regret. Sadly, the greater guilt may actually be ours if we had refused to set a high standard for our children about honesty. What was passed down to us as an axiom from Benjamin Franklin two hundred and fifty years ago is still as true today as it was then: "Honesty is the best policy. Period.

CHEATING

Dishonesty comes in many forms. It is like a trap set to snare us. It entices with the allure of short-term gain, but bites and chews up its victims sooner or later. One of the most insidious realms in which falsehood has gained a foothold is in the academic arena. This is scary, because it means that as each of us passes through the doors of institutions from our youth, we are faced with the temptation to suppress conscience and pervert what is right. Whether our sons and daughters are sheltered from the allurement depends largely on how well we have done and continue to do throughout their growing years to cultivate a truth-loving heart.

In a survey of 24,000 students at 70 American high schools, Donald McCabe (Rutgers University) found that 64 percent of students admitted to cheating on a test, 58 percent admitted to plagiarism and 95 percent said they participated in some form of cheating, whether on a test or plagiarizing or copying homework.[14]

This is not just an American problem. India is a case in point. As reported in Singapore's *The Strait Times*:

India's highest court Monday barred hundreds of students

from becoming doctors after they were caught paying bribes and cheating on exams to gain admission into prestigious medical schools. Around 630 students from central Madhya Pradesh state were found to have copied answers, had proxies sit their exams or just outright paid to gain entry to selective medical colleges between 2008 and 2013.[15]

In recent years, massive cheating scandals have also been reported in China where it had become so out of control that, in 2016, the Chinese government criminalized cheating on the college entrance examinations (called *gaokao*). If caught, the convicted may face up to seven years in prison!

And it is not limited to the *gaokao*. Students start cheating from at a young age, on papers, essays, and other homework assignments, plus exams. As they grow older, the cheating becomes more sophisticated. Hong Kong's *South China Morning Post* published an article with detailed findings:

> It's the SAT, the GRE, and a whole host of other exams. An estimated 90 per cent of all recommendation letters for Chinese applicants to United States universities are fake. Some 70 per cent of application essays are not written by students, and 50 per cent of grades transcripts are falsified.[16]

And it doesn't stop there. Once students arrive in the U.S., there is a thriving black market of cheating services. The author writes, tongue in cheek, "It seems you can get a degree from an Ivy League school without ever having to leave your house!"

What makes us think that the cheating won't continue after graduation? If children are raised to be immune to the toxicity of lying, if they have found a measure of success by playing the system, why would they not just continue to do so in their professional careers, in their relationships, or on their taxes (cheating on taxes cost the U.S. government four-hundred-billion dollars in 2016).[17]

If cheating goes unchecked, kids' play may turn into adults' panic. I have known of cases of people who made false statements on applications for schools and jobs, who were later caught in their lie only to suffer public humiliation. What had taken them years to build, once condemned, came crashing down.

I TRUST YOU

Honesty is not just some ancient virtue, some dusty old precept from the Puritan handbook; it's a foundation for trust and quality relationships. Being honest is not only a good thing to do in case you get caught, or in case the repercussions catch up with you some day. To say that you trust someone 80 percent is an oxymoron. Either you trust someone or you don't. There is no mixture, no half-truth, for a half-truth is the same as an untruth. The point here is, if I want to build positive connections with friends, colleagues, or customers, there is no shortcut. I must believe them, and they must believe me. The moment I am found to be dishonest, that's when I forfeit the relationship-building and relationship-sustaining trust others had in me.

Similarly, when my bride and I stood before each other on our wedding day, we made our vows not because they were a good idea or a ceremonial custom. Vows cannot be obeyed in part, for to break the vow at any point makes it a broken vow. While the words were important, I had to have complete confidence that Joyce spoke with total sincerity and truthfulness. And she had to have the same confidence in me. There had to be unmitigated trust. That's required for building and sustaining relationships.

CONCLUSION

The very fact that being honest conjures up a pious image in many minds today adds particular urgency to this chapter. We live in the hour of "fake news," when even the most reliable institutions have fallen prey to moral decay. Political agendas, blind ambitions, and dog-eat-dog competition on the academic, commercial, or media worlds have all driven us further and further away from this quality so essential to healthy relationships. This is the very thing which stirs us to show our deepest admiration for the Washingtons and Lincolns of yesterday, but which fails to grip our own hearts as necessary or practical for day-to-day living in the present.

We must not be duped. And we must not let our children be duped. Honesty is indeed an ancient concept, you might say as old as the world itself, built into the very fabric of the universe's foundations. It's like a force that keeps the planets in orbit around the sun. If we want stability, consistency, incorruptibility, and permanence in our lives and in the lives of our loved ones, in our homes and our communities, we must insist on personal integrity and transparency. There is simply no substitute for *being honest*.

PUT IT TO WORK

- Have you ever had one of those "raw, candid moments" with your children when you became transparent and vulnerable? When you show the courage to take off your mask, you are showing them that they can, too. **Write down your thoughts on how you can become more vulnerable** (age appropriately) with your children.

- **Read the section on "The Tale of Two Presidents" with your kids.** Use it as a springboard to talk about the relationship of character and greatness.

- **Talk to your children about cheating at school.** Have they ever done it? Do they understand the potential consequences? Do they know of others who have done it? If your son or daughter was failing or struggling and the opportunity arose to cheat, is he or she still confident about doing the right thing?

- **Write an "Honesty Covenant," and have everyone in the family sign it!** Use your own words, but use the following as a guide: *We, as* *members of the _____ family, hereby commit to living our lives with honesty. We will keep our word, and we follow the example of George Washington who said, "Father, I cannot tell a lie." And that means any lie, even a "white lie." We will not cheat even if it means we might get better grades or promotions in life.*

Chapter Four

PEACE, GLORIOUS PEACE

*My son, do not forget my teaching, but keep my
commands in your heart, for they will prolong
your life many years and bring peace and
prosperity.*[18]

— SOLOMON, KING OF ISRAEL, 967 BC

*P*eace is costly, but war is deadly. J. K. Laney in
his book *Marching Orders* writes that during the
last four thousand years of history, there has only been 268
years of peace.[19] Despite man's best efforts, disagreements
grow into conflicts, and conflicts spiral into wars. No trite
pronouncements by sages, idealists, or people with the most
noble of intentions can change this fact. No politician can
rewrite history; no social media effort can erase this land-
scape. If only peace were as easy to keep as it is to desire.

In truth, even when guns are laid down, and the white

flags are raised, a war of a different kind rages on. For as hard as skirmishes over borders or ethnic and racial tensions are to stop, there is a war within our hearts upon which negotiations, compromises, or education has little effect. The weapons engaged are not tanks or jets or even nuclear weapons; they are the jabs upon one's conscience or the stabbing of one's guilt. As hard as it is to achieve world peace, achieving inner peace is an even greater challenge. There is no United Nations for the soul—no North Atlantic Treaty Organization (NATO) for the mind. Yes, this peace is costly, too.

Notice I said *costly,* not *impossible.* The best protection against this kind of attack is not Patriot Missiles or "Star Wars" defense shields. Though Hollywood would decry the thought of such a campaign, I would raise a simple slogan as a formula for achieving the proverbially illusive ideal of peace: *Children, obey your mother and your father.* Sounds archaic, doesn't it? Sounds overly simplistic and naïve, too. But as we mature, as the sphere of our responsibilities broaden, the force of the basic life principle of obedience also grows as we intersect with an increasingly complex web of relationships.

Peace must start at home. It must be woven skillfully into the very fabric of who we are. From there, it extends to school, to the workplace, and to every other area of our lives wherein we are positioned in relationship to those who are in authority.

KID'S STORY (PART 1)

It is one thing for parents to want their children to obey them. It is another when children experience the benefits of obedience for themselves.

Our daughter Elizabeth, who is now twenty-eight, shares two stories on this important matter from when she was eleven and twenty-one.

———

I could see my parents from where I was standing. They were enjoying lunch with some friends, while I stood nervously from afar. I knew I would be interrupting their meeting, but I had just kissed a boy on the cheek and had to get it off my chest. My poor eleven-year-old, guilt-ridden heart couldn't keep it in.

I marched over to where my mom was, quickly whispered my indiscretions in her ear, and turned around to walk away. I immediately felt relief, nervous now only as to what punishment may be meted out.

Looking back now, I'm sure my parents were more amused than upset. My mom later thanked me for my honesty, and gently reminded me that it was too early to be kissing boys.

I do not think I was consciously trying to be a "perfect" kid or a "goody-two-shoes"; I just knew that I couldn't bear doing something I wasn't "supposed" to do. Having a clear conscience appealed to me. The easiest way to do that as a kid was to obey the rules and guidelines set by my parents. Oddly enough, I enjoyed obeying them! It was probably because, deep down, I knew I felt safe in their love for me. I grew to understand that joy was an outcome of an obedient lifestyle, but peace came from knowing that I was deeply loved no matter what.

———

The bedrock of Western civilization is its Judeo-Christian values. More than three thousand years ago, King Solomon wrote that his father David had charged him: Don't forget the things I have taught you, and let your heart keep my commandments. The result? Peace! And that is not all. Peace too has fringe benefits: One's length and quality of life are guaranteed.

Peace is like intravenous chicken soup for the soul. When you have tranquility within yourself, you are anchored to the point that you are not affected by the height or strength of the waves pounding around you. Bombs may fall without, but security reigns within. No wonder the person who has peace lives long and well!

CONSCIENCE

What Solomon and other giants from ancient times referred to in their writings is an unseen entity known as the conscience. We cannot measure conscience with a stethoscope, and an MRI does not capture its reading. But as sure as there is a wind behind the waving of a raised flag, there is a conscience acting as a gauge of peace in the spirit of every one of us.

To what might the conscience be compared? A healthy, clean conscience is like that of a thermostat *which has the power to maintain* a constant and optimal level of comfort inside one's house even though temperatures may rise or fall in extreme conditions outside. Sadly, many have ignored or suppressed conscience to their own hurt. Their inner voice that was meant to be like the thermostat has become more like the thermometer *which can only measure* the rise and fall of temperature but is otherwise powerless to affect any change.

This sentiment is also captured in the quotation of a young German girl who kept a diary during more than two years of hiding in German-occupied Netherlands. She hid with her family in a secret annex behind a bookcase in the office where her father had worked. Anne Frank, who was later recognized as one of *Time* magazine's one hundred most important people of the century, wrote (at the age of thirteen) in her diary, *"A quiet conscience makes one strong!"*[20] She had witnessed people, at that time, throw away their conscience, and with it their peace, betraying others or joining the side of the Nazis for what they imagined would give them security. She had also witnessed those who chose to obey their consciences and risked their lives for the sake of total strangers, harboring them, or joining an underground movement to provide sanctuary for other innocent people.

One such person was Casper Ten Boom. He was Corrie Ten Boom's father. His home was a sanctuary for hundreds of Jews whose lives were spared through this family's courage. Upon arrest, Casper, then eighty-five, was offered the opportunity to return home in peace, to which he coolly replied, "If I go home today . . . tomorrow I will open my door again to any man in need who *knocks.*"[21]

Daddy Ten Boom understood something that may be one of the best legacies we can ever pass on to our children: Only as we set a watchman over our consciences will we ever know the meaning of true and lasting harmony. For Casper, to turn someone away was to admit defeat and to deny the voice reverberating inside his heart. Though he may have lived, something deep on the inside would have died.

REWARDS VS. REGRETS

Parents who recognize the power of the conscience in nurturing peace in their children will bring correction when their children do not obey quickly and will provide appropriate rewards when their children spontaneously do the things parents have instructed. Once this pattern of obedience to parental instructions is established, the children will naturally become more joyful. I have seen children who accept the constraint of an established bedtime go to bed happy and wake up happy. And I have also seen children who struggle with this "rule" not only waste time when their bodies should have been resting, but when their minds could have been rejuvenated as well. They end up struggling to their own hurt.

The same is true of children who obey their parents' instruction to do their homework in a timely manner. They finish their work and are able to devote more time to doing things that are fun, or they have time to pursue an interest or enjoy connecting with a friend. By contrast, when a child develops a habit of procrastinating, they can fall prey to an anxiety-filled life of always rushing to finish things or hurrying to get to where they need to go at the last minute.

The consequences of disobedience over a lifetime are deeper than just a lack of personal peace. Disobedience can lead to strife, to lack of discipline, to becoming increasingly desensitized to the inner guide of the conscience, and to a blurred sense of right and wrong. Relationships can be adversely affected, as disobedience can lead you down the slippery slope of shame and broken communication. A child who thinks disobedience doesn't have consequences risks waking up when he is older wishing he had some way to remove the weight of guilt and regret that is on his shoulders.

In modern times, *submission* is almost considered a dirty word. It carries with it an image of being enslaved, or coerced, or pacified. This is most unfortunate. It did not always have such a negative image. Submission literally means to place oneself under (sub-) the mission of another, which assumes that the mission is a progressive, moving together towards the accomplishment of a purpose. Submission, in its traditional use, described the positive response of one person to another *from the heart*.

As a parent, my goal cannot be only to get my children to do what I ask them to do. If they obey me in bitterness or frustration, I may have lost a battle that on the surface seemed like I had won. So, my goal is to develop the right heart attitude in my sons and daughters for which obeying is a natural product.

Submission, properly understood, is the ardent response of a heart that aims to please another. Though it is hard to paint this word without the colors of twenty-first-century bias, I am hoping, in fact, that my children will submit to their mother and me.

As parents we should soberly weigh our roles and our methods, however, to move our children toward submission and obedience. This chapter is not a license for you to be a dictator! If teaching your children to obey you as their parent is conducted in a demanding or aggressive manner, you may gain their outward assent while creating an inward resentment. This will not yield peace; it may even produce anger or rebellion. Our opening proverb combines the idea of "commanding" with instruction, which means we tell them *what* to do (which is for their own good), as well as *why* and *how* they should do it.

Ideally, we should provide guidance to our children about a matter before we ask them to do it. But there are also times when I have required my children's obedience without the benefit of teaching them about the matter first. In such cases, I will find the time *later* to come back to this subject and explain to them why such a demand was necessary. This gives rise to heartfelt loyalty that is life-giving, rather than clench-fist "obedience" that is a harbinger of relational peril.

KID'S STORY (PART 2)

Here is the second part of our Elizabeth's story:

———

Many years later, I had another talk with my parents about

a different boy. (Let's call him *Adam*.) Usually, I kept my crushes to myself. Most of the time, it was because I knew deep down inside that those boys, though not "bad boys" per se, were probably not marriage material either. Also, I was a teenager at the time, so even if they were marriage material, I wasn't marrying age anyways. But Adam was different (something I'm sure we can all admit to saying at some point in our lives). He was very respectful towards me, servant-hearted towards those around him, passionate about the people he loved and his dreams, and incredibly fun to top it all off. I was twenty-one at the time, and I really, really thought that this guy was "the one." We had been through close to three years of friendship at that point, and compared to every other guy I had met, he was hands-down the most incredible of them all. The only thing was my parents were not convinced.

I struggled with that. I struggled with them. I struggled with God. I thought, *No! Perhaps my parents just need a little more time. They'll see what I see and grow to love him as well.* Three years of friendship passed, and my parents did not change their minds. To cut a long story short, I walked away from my precious friendship with Adam twice on account of what my parents prayed and felt. The first time was hard enough, but the second time? I was devastated and heartbroken. I remember going to bed that night, afraid to fall asleep because I knew that I would wake up the next morning and Adam would no longer be in my life.

Up until that point, I had benefited from obeying my parents. I trusted and believed them explicitly—no questions asked—and as a result I had led a blessed life throughout my childhood and teen years. Mom and Dad seemed to know best, even if I didn't always understand their ways. However, this time it seemed different. I was sure they were biased in their regards towards Adam, and I was on the receiving end. *Surely my parents weren't always right, right?* I had thought. Regardless, I made the difficult choice to end my friendship with Adam anyways. But unlike my childhood and teenage years, I knew that I had to start learning how to discern right from wrong, and wise from foolish, when making decisions. I could not go through life asking my parents about every decision, especially if I wanted to be a good parent myself one day.

Parents lay the foundation of peace and obedience for their children, not only so that they may experience a pain-free upbringing, but as a pattern to follow when they have their own families in the future. It's a legacy that passes from parents to their children, and their children's children. This particular story tells of a pivotal time for me. Most of my friends had already been making their own decisions for a long time (especially when it came to whom they could and could not date), and heeding my parents' instruction so "late" in life was certainly not the norm.

Today, I am married. And my husband Anthony is far beyond anything I could have ever imagined in all my years of daydreaming and journal entries. And as wonderful as Adam was, he was not "the one for me." I wouldn't be where I am today if it were not for the safety, love, and peace that came from obeying my parents. Everyone grows up "obeying" someone or something (money, love, themselves, etc.). Discerning whom or what to believe and obey when one is older is a lot more difficult if one did not learn to obey his or her parents and reap the blessings as a kid.

———

NO RULES?

Not all children are so willing to follow the safety of their parents' guidance. "No rules" is a slogan which dawned on young people's T-shirts and skateboards, and was popularized on music videos and even a movie by this name. Many youth around the world naïvely ascribe to a belief that rules are a form of restraint that restrict their freedoms. Ironically, these same youths may gather to watch the Super Bowl or the World Cup without drawing a parallel that no one would be tuning in if either one of these games had no rules! It's a parody to think anyone would be interested to play or watch a game where a ball was thrown into the middle of a field for two groups of people just to throw and kick willy nilly! In truth, the games are a reflection of what life in the real world is like.

The same is true of rules that apply to our road systems. I have had the privilege of living in many countries and among many cultures. But this has not always translated to a sense of enjoyment when I have had to drive. In some places, drivers routinely pass on blind curves or create a third lane (where there were only two) in order to avoid head-on collisions. In others, traffic signs are interpreted as "suggestions" by many drivers, which means they might as well not exist! In several nations, I have also witnessed how drivers will all squeeze into any available space at intersections, seemingly unaware that by doing so they have created a logjam, whereby neither they nor any other vehicles will be able to move at all! In my homeland, I have driven ten thousand miles in a month and never seen an accident. In one place I stayed, I saw accidents two or three times in a week driving a mile back and forth to pick up my daughter from school!

I wish I could communicate to drivers in these settings that rules of the road are a good thing. When everyone obeys them, driving is so much more pleasant, stress-free, and safe! When other drivers stay in their lanes, I am not constantly on the lookout for when they are going to swipe me. When they keep a safe distance behind me, I can keep my eyes ahead, where they are supposed to be, rather than anxiously on the rearview mirror. I shouldn't need to panic when lanes merge, when I come to an intersection, or when someone is passing me as though they were playing the newest, high-speed video game! Obeying traffic regulations brings order and peace to me, to the other drivers, and to pedestrians.

I also wish I could communicate to all youth that the rules that we as parents have set are meant to be for their good. Obeying Mom and Dad is designed to lead children down the road of life, arriving safely at each and every destination. The idea that a game can be played without rules is fantasy. The idea that people could just get in their cars and ignore traffic laws is dangerous. The idea that a family can happily function without rules is impractical.

SMOOTH SAILING

What do the "roads" of your household look like? Over the years, many people have commented that they feel a calmness and serenity in our home. Although we have worked hard to lay a solid foundation through instruction, correction, and discipline, the long-term benefits far outweigh any perceived cost.

One couple traveled with us for two weeks and said they were amazed that our children got along the whole time. Riding on trains, carrying luggage, standing in lines, and squeezing into cabs, there were plenty of opportunities for a temper to flare or patience to run thin. But our children did not argue with each other or have a spat with us the whole time!

In reality, peace begets peace. When two people are at peace within themselves, they are much less likely to fight with each other. When I stay in my lane and don't encroach on others, the chance of an accident or the occurrence of road rage decreases dramatically.

When our children discover that submission brings a blessing, they will want to pass it along to their families some day. Obedience is one thing that everyone has the same access to, for it is ultimately a choice. Submission cannot be coerced. But whoever has learned to live by it obtains peace.

There was also the time when we went on a working "road trip." We traveled in an eight-seater van with six of our children, ages one through eighteen, for five weeks, covering twelve thousand miles and staying in a different bed almost every night. How did we survive, you might ask?

My first answer would be that we just have great kids. We also did mix in some days of fun along the way, which helped. But on those long days of driving, hot and cramped in the car, the fact that we were able to maintain our sanity was certainly not simply a coincidence or luck, for that matter. While we are far from perfect parents, and none of our children have halos that we have been able to detect, from the time they were young, we have nurtured peace in their hearts, the product of obedience. That is why I truly hope you are able to cultivate it in your home as well.

CONCLUSION

Finally, when we have passed on the value of obedience and of keeping our consciences clear, we have not only released the potential of peace in a heart, we are preparing the next generation to become good citizens. Lessons learned in relating to parents are then repeated when our children are called to relate to teachers, to bosses, to police, to government, or to anyone who is in authority. Obedience will also serve them well when they get married!

When they are taught to recognize and heed the voice of conscience, they are garnering the qualities by which the conscience of a community is stimulated. Or in the words of one of the wisest sages of the twentieth century, Russian dissident and author Aleksandr Solzhenitsyn: "Those who clearly recognize the voice of their own conscience usually recognize also the voice of justice."[22]

Maybe this is why the voice of justice is also being silenced in so many corners of our world today. When justice is trampled on in our streets, listen for the drum-beats of war, for they cannot be far behind.

If peace is to be *attained* and then *maintained*, obedience must be incubated in the hearts of our children from the beginning.

When our children harken to the voice of our instructions, they are not just doing so for us—to appease us somehow. If the path we lead them down does not come with guard- and hand-rails, steps and markers, it may become a slippery slope barreling down towards shame and frustration. The alternative, the road of compliance and willingness to follow our teaching and guidance, leads them to a verdant spot in a meadow clearing, where a spring-fed pool bids them come and drink.

PUT IT TO WORK

- **Talk to your kids about the "little voice inside,"** better known as the conscience (Elizabeth spoke of her "poor eleven-year-old, guilt-ridden heart"). Talk about the difference between a thermostat and a thermometer. Which one do we want our conscience to act like?

- Maybe there is something that your son or daughter has done wrong for which he or she is feeling a weight of guilt. **Encourage him or her to talk** about it so that it does not fester and become a regret, or worse.

- Are you as a parent *forcing* your children to obey? **Honestly assess your methods.** Ask yourself, *Do I strike a balance of "commanding" with instruction as Solomon said?* Are you not only telling them *what* to do, but *why* and *how* as well?

- In the age of "No Rules" pop culture, **discuss the effects of no rules in real life** (e.g., if your kids play a sport, it would be a good place to start).

Chapter Five

KNIGHTS TO REMEMBER

You will never do anything in this world without courage. It is the greatest quality of the mind next to honor.[23]

— ARISTOTLE

"Hey, Tom. Hi, Mary. I'm home."

I'd gone to my friend Eric's house. When he walked into the house and greeted Tom and Mary, I wondered who they were. I knew that he did not have any siblings with these names. So who were they? Just then, his mom came around the corner. I was shocked to learn that her name was Mary. And then I discovered Tom was Eric's father. *How could he possibly call them by their first names?!* I thought to myself.

I have never been a fan of trends that trivialize the parent/child relationship. I want my children to feel like they can come to me any time they have a need. I want them to be able to take me into their confidence. I want them to feel like they can totally be themselves around me. I want us to have things that we can do in common—things that are fun! While these are all things which are shared between friends, that does not mean my children and I are thereby "friends" in the same way that a classmate or a neighbor is. I am their father, and that means there may be some characteristics of our relationship similar to what friends have, but ours will always be more, much more.

In contrast to the "Tom and Mary" experience, I remember the first time I was in the home of a marvelous family I deeply respected in the Southern U.S. To my shock, the children addressed their mom and dad as Ma'am and Sir! While foreign to my Northern U.S. ears, I could not deny that there was not something melodious about this. The family exhibited a lot of peace and order. They were happy, hospitable, and generous. Years later, this family has continued to have a significant impact on their community, and as the kids have grown up and spread out, they have carried the same energy and kindly footprint with them wherever they have gone.

While addressing Mom and Dad as Ma'am and Sir is certainly no magic formula, there is something fundamentally right about what I had witnessed in the Southern family. It may be a coincidence that the other family, Eric's family, later became a broken one, but I have come to understand that there is an ingredient which is never missing from a healthy family, and that is honor.

We use the title *Doctor* before our physician's last name. We call our judges *Your Honor*. And we don't forget to call the man—with the five prominent stars on his uniform directly above row after row of medals—*General.* These titles are earned, and to overlook their importance would be a violation of more than just verbal protocol. When we reject the values of honor and respect under the banner of progress, we do so to our own hurt.

THE LACK OF HONOR

Not too long ago, I was listening intently to a lecturer, entranced by his breakdown and analysis of some of the trends and symptoms that are affecting our institutions, and some of the ways in which our traditions are being eroded. Then he said something that was both climactic and pinpointed in its accuracy: "The common thread linking all of these is the lack of honor!" Scales fell from my eyes. I suddenly realized that this well-known author had hit the proverbial nail on the head. There is a cancer that is crying out for a diagnosis and cure in our world today; it has to do with something we have lost, and that thing is honor.

It is almost as though the word *honor* has been bleached from our vocabulary. How did we find such a powerful eraser? What kind of a mystical wand has been waved to make this "rabbit in the hat" disappear? Honor has been a part of the fabric of great civilizations for millennia! Honor was enshrined as the highest virtue in the teachings of Confucius, whose philosophy has singularly impacted all the major cultures of the East. Likewise, the great Greek philosophers like Socrates, Plato, and Aristotle, whose thoughts cannot be separated from Western civilization, also espoused honor as a paramount virtue. Among the Ten Commandments is the injunction, "Honor your father and your mother, that your days may be long upon the land which the Lord your God is giving you."[24]

The pages of history—East and West, North and South—are inked with personalities who framed our moral structures with their pens or our conquests with their swords. They are judged not just by their deeds, brilliance, or exploits, but whether they were honorable. Honor is the dividing line, helping people throughout history answer this question: Should we follow this one or not?

Some personalities are remembered for what they have done—like Hitler or Stalin. Some are remembered for who they were—like Gandhi or Jesus. Some are infamous, while others are famous, and whether they were honorable is the plumb line that either condemns or eulogizes, repels or attracts.

You won't find any books on the *New York Times* Best Seller list these days on the topic of honor. In our arrogance, indeed our ignorance, our modern minds are convinced that we have moved past such archaic, Camelot concepts. Imagining ourselves wise, we really ought to compare ourselves to fools who in their shortsighted naïveté gorge themselves with junk food, consuming potato chips, chocolate, and Coca Cola week after week, year after year. Pimples, rotting teeth, obesity, and premature death are all going to catch up with us sooner or later. It's cause and effect. Our moral diet affects our behavior sooner or later just as our food choice affects our health.

THE KAEPERNICK EFFECT

The most "famous" athlete in America in 2017 never touched a ball or ran a race. And yet, Colin Kaepernick was selected as the runner-up in *Time* magazine's Person of the Year and awarded the *Sports Illustrated* Sportsperson of the Year. His accomplishment? He is considered heroic for inspiring protests against racial inequalities, though his method was to refuse to comply with the rule and tradition of standing for the playing of the U.S. National Anthem before the start of the game. Many were incensed.

In previous generations, and among a large percentage of the population of American citizens today, this would be deemed unpatriotic, even sacrilegious. We never would have celebrated such irreverent behavior in times past. What has happened?

Like the "h" in the word itself, the call for honor has become silent. When I was young, we had a deep respect for people in uniform, whether our soldiers armed to defend our nation or our police deployed to keep our streets safe. This morning, in news which has now become commonplace, one of the headlines was of French youth posting a video of them laughing while pulverizing a policewoman whom they had lured into a trap so they could senselessly kick and beat her.

When I was young, every student in every school would stand facing the flag with their hands on their hearts to say the "Pledge of Allegiance." Pupils did not talk back to and challenge their teachers. Television news debates and coverage followed a standard of etiquette. There was no swearing on air, discourse was civil, and tempers restrained.

People who held office or positions of authority, or who had sacrificed greatly in our history to uphold our freedoms and way of life, were esteemed. Honor, like the monuments and statues erected to commemorate these men and women, is now facing increasing calls to be torn down.

These sentiments are more than just "good ol' days," nostalgic musings. Backstage, there is a much more sinister plot unfolding. People are less grateful. Attitudes have turned critical, conversations more rude and crude. Violent and aggressive actions have become a natural product of this dismantling spiral.

As standards have fallen and tolerance of impropriety has risen, a phoenix may be rising out of the ashes as modern-day prophets are beginning to identify and speak to the heart of what has been lost. Consider these words penned by Larry Stockstill, author of *Model Man*:

> I've been really concerned about the lack of honor in our nation. On vacation recently, my wife saw a veteran walk out on to the beach in the pouring rain with lightning flashing everywhere and wind howling. He walked over to a flagpole where an American flag was flapping in the breeze. He stood in the rain, put his hand over his heart, saluted, and respectfully took the flag down to safety inside. This is HONOR. It means to respect what something (or someone) represents. That flag did not represent a piece of fabric flailing in the rainstorm. It represented millions of American men and women who gave their blood on foreign battlefields to birth, defend, and protect this great nation.[25]

We as parents are going to need a lot of courage, and wisdom, to resurrect honor in our homes and communities in the face of such threats.

HONORING AT HOME

The unraveling of the principle and practice of honor in cultures around the world does not mean that we cannot reap the benefits of a "mutual admiration society" at home. But it means we are going to have to fight harder to recover it.

The ancient Greek philosophers may not have had smartphones, but their brilliance has been a bedrock of thought on which great civilizations, and families, have arisen. Confucius's teachings were very practical and focused on a handful of relationships. The family was the primary place where our morals were to be learned and put into practice, and then from this core fan out to affect our responses of submission or duty to those outside the home—from friends to officers, all the way up to the emperor.

The Bible not only commands children to honor their parents, it similarly says that wives are to honor their husbands, husbands to honor their wives, and all are to honor our elders. It calls us to honor those in authority and, specifically, to honor the king.

So how do we show honor? First of all, it may be helpful to understand the difference between honor and respect. Although they may be used interchangeably, honor is related to position, whereas respect is produced when another has performed in a way that is admirable or appropriate. Honor is generally given; respect typically earned.

Just because I honor a group of soldiers for their willingness to give their lives to defend my freedom, that does not mean I have to respect them when they are uncouth or belligerent. When I respect others, I am bringing them to a place of equal footing, so in this sense respect is also in some manner given (not earned), though not to the same degree as honor. Out of respect, I allow others to speak as I would want to be given the opportunity to speak. But when I honor another, I am giving preference to him or her. I shake a hand out of respect. I bow a knee out of honor.

Ideally, the person to whom I am rendering honor has also earned my respect. But honor must be maintained. When I don't agree with some laws that are instituted under an administration, I still have to honor and uphold these laws even when I don't have a high regard for the lawmakers. In a game such as basketball, both teams must honor the referees and, by extension, the calls and judgments they make. Though the ref in my present game is considered to have done poorly in a previous match, if the teams use this as a basis to resist or argue, even the ability to play the game breaks down. Presidents, police, principals, and parents all need to be honored—period. If the game breaks down when there is no honor, what about our societies or our homes?

I am fortunate to have parents and a wife who are not only deserving of my honor, but who are also worthy of my respect. But what about the case when respect has not been earned? That is when my commitment to honor kicks in.

I had been on my own and financially independent for a few years when I faced a decision by which my parents were not directly impacted. Though my culture told me it was my decision to make, I deferred to a voice deep inside that was telling me to honor my parents in this matter. I determined that I would not do this thing unless they gave me their blessing. Looking back, I can see where this was a protection to me. And now that some of my children have grown, I find that they also honor me in this same way. I am grateful.

The ancients were more than wise; they were tapped in to an immutable truth—honor your mother and father. God finished inscribing this command with His own finger on those tablets of stone He gave to Moses with a delicious promise, "so that you may live a long time."

Rachel from the Philippines learned the value of honor early in life. She wrote:

———

I was three or four when my mom got me a voice teacher. I loved singing at parties and at home, so my parents decided that I would start having voice lessons to improve my singing.

I remember being excited about my first lesson. I sang for my teacher, and we did some vocalizing. It was a bit of fun, so I continued having lessons. By the time I was seven, singing had become boring.

It was the same routine every week: going to lessons, vocalizing, singing the song we were currently learning, and going back home. I didn't enjoy singing anymore. My parents really wanted me to sing in front of an audience, but at that time I was really shy. I refused profusely.

I wanted to stop having lessons because I didn't think my voice was improving anyways. I wanted to give up my singing, but my parents didn't let me stop my lessons. I was really frustrated and disappointed because I felt like I was wasting my time. I even remember not being able to speak for weeks after my tonsillectomy for my sleep apnea. I thought that that would finally be the time I stopped my lessons, but my mom made sure I continued my lessons.

Here's the thing with honoring your parents: If you do honor them, you get to reap the blessings. I persevered through my lessons and found my voice. Now, I sing broadway and opera at the age of thirteen.

But what if you don't honor your parents? When I was around eight or nine, my family went on a trip to Canada. We visited many places, including Montreal. We were having dinner in a fancy restaurant that had a mini balcony that was only around a couple feet high. My parents told me to be careful while I played there with my other cousins. I did not honor them by being disobedient. I was not careful and ended up falling off the balcony when I sat on the ledge of the railings. I hit my head on the concrete sidewalk, and I was helped back up by a stranger.

Not honoring your parents has its consequences. I realized this when I got a contusion from the fall. I was constantly dizzy, and it was hard for me to walk straight. This happened to me because I was foolish, and I did not listen to my parents. I learned that honoring your parents is good for you. It will benefit you in many ways. Your parents know and want the best for you, so you should trust and obey them.

———

BADGES AND SALUTES

Men and women in military service put their lives on the line for each other and for people whom they will never meet or see, every day. Perhaps that is why the military is one of the remaining places where the *culture of honor* is still strictly adhered to today. It can't afford to break down.

According to the U.S. Army, of all the values, honor is the one that embodies all the others. Honor is a matter of carrying out, acting, and living the values of respect, duty, loyalty, selfless service, integrity, and personal courage in everything you do.

It's this sense of honor that moved the veteran to collect the flag in a torrential downpour with lightning crashing. It's this sense of honor that causes a man to brave oncoming bullets above and landmines beneath in order to rescue a wounded platoon mate. It's honor that holds him back when everything in his mind is screaming it is the perfect time to run into the fray, but his sergeant has yet to give the command.

Here are some excerpts from the Army's Code of Honor:

- We demonstrate honor by doing the honorable thing, even when no one is around to witness it, and striving to do the right thing at all times.

- "Having honor defines you to others. . . . If you have honor, you are a known quantity and therefore can be trusted."

- Honor is critical to the success of an organization

and is an important ingredient in enhancing mission accomplishment. When you come to work focused on the mission and the betterment of all those you work with and serve, you are demonstrating and exemplifying honor.

- Honor is also a commitment—a commitment to standing behind what you say and do and by simply doing the right thing with no expectation of reward or praise.[26]

What nation, company, organization, or family would not benefit greatly from having a commitment to such a code as this?!

KNIGHTS IN SHINING ARMOR

One of the other conspicuous times when the concept of honor was prominent was during the Age of Chivalry. Romanticized in the tales and legends surrounding the likes of King Arthur, the culture, class, heroism, and virtue of the knights have inspired books, movies, and dreams ever since.

Like the Army's Code, these knights and gentlewomen ascribed to a code of conduct called *chivalry*. Enshrining six primary virtues, the crowning virtue again was honor. The loss of honor was considered to be a greater humiliation to a man's standing, worse than death itself. As one of their own expressed so poignantly: "For myself I prefer to hold a little piece of land in honor, than to hold a great empire with dishonor."[27]

The examples of soldiers and knights show us that it is

important to have a code or a commitment to uphold ethical standards and conduct. At its core, Confucianism identified roles and clearly defined expectations for how we should act in these roles towards others within the family. While clarifying standards, roles, and expectations is important, we overlook the most powerful lesson in all of this if we only insist on ascription to a code.

Being a soldier or becoming a knight is a mentality. It is not about doing the right things; it is about who you become when you are a soldier or a knight. The most effective recruiting slogan in U.S. history was the one used when I was in my late teens (and until I turned forty). It was, "Be All You Can Be." The emphasis was on *being*. It is about becoming a certain kind of person, a person of dignity, a person who embodies discipline and commitment.

The same is true of the knighthood. A knight in training adopted the code of conduct, true, but the goal was to become a person of honor. After years of training—of proving oneself as a person of character and prowess, of performing with excellence in jousts, duels, and tournaments—one was recognized with great pomp and ceremony and elevated to the status of a knight, of being called "Sir" (for women the title would be "Lady"), a title one is bestowed for life. The ceremony was called an *accolade*.

Here is the principle: We as parents have to do more than simply demand honor. We need to define honor, establish standards, and most importantly, we need to create a culture of honor in our homes.

I am "king" of my castle. My goal is to raise my kids not just to honor me, but to be honorable and to reflect a code of excellence. The language of chivalry is of nobles and lords, gentlemen and gentlewomen, titles of dignity and distinction. My aim is to knight my children as sirs and ladies, to dub them with the sword of truth, and to give them their suit of shining armor. The honor that is produced is not merely lip-service, but it's an outworking of who they are from the heart, and it's a quality that is perfected over their lifetimes.

PARENTS SHOWING HONOR

An honoring culture starts with us as parents. Lessons in the home that bring transformation in life are validated and empowered by example. It cannot be a "do as I say but not what I do"situation. Otherwise, our lofty goals and hopes will` fall flat. Our children will know honor not simply because we require it, teach it, or attempt to cultivate it. They will know it because they see it with their own eyes being modeled by us.

If I do not honor my wife, and my wife does not honor me, I am like a noisy gong or a clanging cymbal. If I speak disparagingly about my nation's leaders or complain about people in authority, I have just cut the legs out from under any message about honor that I had hoped to pass on to my own children. If I do not exemplify a genuineness and fervency in entertaining guests, showing regard for the waitress at a restaurant, or being gracious to the neighbors who ride the elevator with us, I risk appearing hypocritical. If I do not honor my own parents, I do not contact them often, I do not support them in times of need, or I do not engage them in our family affairs, my words to my sons and daughters will not carry weight and will fall on deaf ears.

CONCLUSION

In an age when the virtue of honor is being neglected, a time when institutions and traditions are being delegitimized and confronted, it is vital that we don't throw up our hands in surrender to winds and waves of popular culture. The excesses of a few have actually alerted the world that values which have long sustained civilizations of the East and West are under threat.

The Age of Chivalry may have passed, but the need for a code of honor has not. As parents, let us seize the opportunity to redeem one of the most important qualities that will make our society and our households strong. Build a culture of honor in your home. Raise your kids with a respect for institutions and for those who provide us with leadership and protection. Instill in them the values and the characteristics that are consistent with nobility. Though dark clouds may dot the horizon, I am going to do my part to extend the sword over my sons and daughters and clothe them in shining armor.

PUT IT TO WORK

- **Ask your kids to define "honor."** I mention that something like "scales fell from my eyes" when the lecturer I was listening to spoke about the lack of honor as being one of the keys to understanding the changes that are happening in our world today. Mention a couple ways of how showing honor has changed since the time when you were young.

- **Read the paragraph on the difference between honor and respect.** Ask the kids to talk about people whom they respect in their lives and why. Whom do they honor? Why?

- **Ask the following question:** "Would you have gone out in the rain to collect the flag in a downpour? Why or why not?"

- There are many versions of the story of King Arthur. **Either read a book or watch a movie together** that portrays the story. Discuss what was learned about having a code of honor.

Part Two

DOG QUALITIES

Dogs are best known for their undying loyalty. "Man's best friend" is the most relational of all God's creatures, a good reminder to us that, at the end of the day, what we should value most in life is each other. These qualities are gained through quality time spent together: imitation, wisdom, embracing traditions, and friendship.

Chapter Six

"I WANT TO BE JUST LIKE YOU"

In a study of American adolescents, the Search
Institute found that 72 percent of adopted
adolescents wanted to know why they were
adopted, 65 percent wanted to meet their birth
parents, and 94 percent wanted to know which
birth parent they looked like.[28]

— AMERICAN ADOPTION CONGRESS

1996

I remember thinking when I was young that my father was the fastest person in the world. I thought he was the smartest, too. It is just a part of our makeup as children, that we naturally and innocently believe that our own fathers are awesome. Although I never actually saw my father fly over a tall building, I would not have been surprised to discover a super suit hanging in his closet.

Fortunately for me, Dad never smashed my image of his being a man worthy of my adoration and respect.

Then, when I became a father, I realized that my own children would also hold me in high esteem. I discovered my boys would have an innate desire to want to be like me. This awareness has kept me sober, cautious not to violate their sacred trust. Although far from perfect, and wholly unworthy of my hero status, I have worked hard to give my kids a good example to follow and a reason to bear the family name with honor. Hopefully, they will do the same for their kids one day. We parents owe it to our children, not just to leave them an inheritance of silver and gold that passes away but to bequeath them a good name that can never be taken from them.

SHE LOOKS LIKE YOU!

Only recently, I have become a grandparent, and it has to be one of the most blissful and extraordinary things that one can experience in life. Due to the glories of modern technology, my wife and I receive new pictures every day of our little angel. And with each shot comes the natural urge to compare her to others in our family. We say things like, "She has her Aunt Lizzie's chin," "Her nose looks more Chinese," "Her forehead comes from Grandma's side of the family," or "She looks most like you, Grandpa." (Ah, now you're talking!)

There is something comforting, even energizing, about knowing that our children, or our grandchildren, take after us. When anyone gets within striking distance of me these days, I have the photos ready for viewing. I even want to tell strangers. Immediately, a warm smile graces their faces as well. How can anyone resist the sweetness and innocence of a newborn?

As babies grow into toddlers, and toddlers become younger children, the fascination with lookalike features may die down, but the desire for likeness does not. We see in them a reflection of ourselves. We see characteristics, traits, or behaviors. We want to pass on our values and beliefs. In those times when we see our weaknesses and imperfections acted out in them, we are reminded of the grave responsibility we have to be an example, to live a life worth emulating.

As our offspring continue to mature, our hopes and dreams for them take shape. Their personalities and interests surface. Character is formed. They interact with peers and have an ever-widening circle of social networks. In all these things, we still look for ourselves in our children. Their achievement becomes our achievement, their success, our success, their struggle, ours as well.

Finally, our children develop skills and pursue their studies and careers. As they move on, they move out. Though interaction and intersection are less frequent, we now hear from teachers—or friends or future spouses— words that have gripped us from those cradle days: "You know she's a lot like you."

From their early days through the passage of time, I have discovered something: Our playful musings about our children's noses, eyes, and chins as newborns are actually an expression of something wholesome and profound. Something of us has been stamped onto the lives of our descendants. That is both a sobering and a thrilling thought—one that I hope will not lead to embarrassment but to those same proud, grin-filled emotions I enjoy right now as I ponder how my granddaughter "looks like me."

WHAT'S IN A NAME?

Joyce and I carefully chose the names of each of our children. We considered the things we felt would be part of their characteristics or destinies. We anticipated their arrival into this world and understood, from those first moments and throughout their lifetimes, their names would be inseparable from whom they would become.

We also chose to pass on to them a sense of pride in our "family" name or their surname. I told and continue to tell them to consider that our name has been kept honorable by our imperfect, yet hardworking and selfless, forefathers. It has been laid up for them as a non-material inheritance. I have underscored the fact that all that has come to them from this name would not be tarnished by them but be made more respectable by their contribution.

A good name, that's one of the things we want to give our children. It has a power to open doors of opportunity. A bad name will quickly close others. Imagine being given the name Osama when you were born (probably before 2001!) or having Hitler as a family name! When I went to a chiropractor's office and was told the new assistant's name was Bruce Lee (李小龙), I could not help but imagine him performing adjustments using martial arts. I sat outside in the waiting room, expecting to hear the primal scream!

The association of a name can be neutral, but it may also be positive as well as negative. Whichever reputation it may have, without a doubt, there is something in a name!

When William Shakespeare's Juliet said, "What's in a name?" she believed that the last name of her lover, who was from a feuding family, would be of no consequence to their relationship. Unfortunately, her idealism was shattered when the climax of the story ended in tragedy precisely because there *was* something in the name!

I am not advocating judging or rejecting people on the basis of their names. The point here is simply practical: Names can have a powerful effect on people in a good or a bad way. That is why you have probably met many people with the names Peter or John, but none who are called Judas!

I may not leave a large inheritance of lands, houses, or profitable businesses to my children, but I can pass on something even more valuable: a good name. Therefore, I strive to guard and promote the reputation of our family name. I want it to "smell as sweet" as a rose. How about you?

KEEPING IT ROYAL

People who are born into royalty are taught to think and act like those who are set apart and, well, special. From the time they take their first steps, they are taught to walk with a certain gait. As they begin to speak, they are taught the proper way to talk. They are educated in the history and traditions of their royal lineage and are taught principles of honor and duty. They learn about etiquette and are introduced to high culture. Theirs is a world of boundaries and disciplines, where titles such as "Your Highness" or "Your Grace" are used.

Queen Elizabeth II, for example, embodies the essence of elegance in her bearing and dress. She is esteemed by many, and her name is synonymous with service as the longest-reigning British monarch. If she even comes down with a common cold, the world's newspapers are sure to keep an international delegation of loyalists in the know about her condition.

It is little wonder, then, that in all history, the two most watched weddings were of Prince William and Kate Middleton, and Prince Charles and Diana Spencer. These were *long* weddings! But I will never forget the impression I had of how the children in the wedding parties, raised in the shadow of the throne of Great Britain, kept their composure and carried themselves in a dignified manner throughout the ceremonies. Those little ones did not only have a **royal name**; they were given a **royal identity**. No one simply could have warned those young boys and girls, "OK, you are going to be on TV for all the world to see, so be on your best behavior!" and that warning in itself keep the children from behaving like, well, children. Something more was at work there. The children did not only know what to do, their actions and attitudes showed that they had a royal awareness or consciousness, as it were. Some things just cannot be rehearsed.

My father was not a king. I am not the head of a tribe, and no one in my family line has ever had a title of distinction. But my wife and I have imagined our children to be "royal," and so we have been intentional in teaching each of them to have self-respect and to bear the mark of a person of excellence and character. One of the keys to this has been to train each child about who and whose he or she is, not just *what to do.*

Joyce and I have secured our children in their identities as *our* children in *our* family with a good heritage. Then, we directed their focus on *being* and not only on *doing,* making a healthy identity and not simply "right behavior" as the goal.

THE LEGACY OF JONATHAN EDWARDS

An inspirational example of a man who endowed his descendants with a royal consciousness, yet was himself not of royal ancestry, is Jonathan Edwards. He is known as the father of the Great Awakening. He lived during a period in early American history (beginning in the 1720s) when moral decay and apathy had a darkening influence on society. During the awakening, people suddenly, and in large numbers, were being roused from spiritual slumber. They were being called to account for their actions, and the impact in lowering crime and strengthening family bonds is well documented.[29]

Generations later, an American educator by the name of A. E. Winship researched one hundred and fifty years of Edwards' descendants only to make an astounding discovery. Jonathan Edwards' progeny included: 1 Vice-President of the United States, 3 U.S. Senators, 3 governors, 3 mayors, 13 college presidents, 30 judges, 65 professors, 80 public office holders, 100 lawyers, and 100 missionaries.[30] This is both sobering and heartening at the same time.

As parents, we can unleash tremendous potential in our

children, and our children's children, to achieve monu-
mental success into the distant future. We can also fail to
live a life worth following and leave the results to chance.

LOOKALIKES

When our third daughter turned twenty, Joyce and I brought
her with us for a trip over the weekend. After a brief intro-
duction to our friends or associates, a discussion would
often ensue when they would comment about the ways in
which she resembled me and the other ways in which she
was more like her mother. The most touching remarks were
those in which others said she was a combination of the
best features of both of us. Joyce and I were greatly moved
by that.

There are few things more satisfying than hearing others
say your children have grown up and "look like you." It
reminds us as parents that our children are uniquely a
product and extension of our lives together. If it were not
for our love—the love shared between us their parents—our
sons and daughters would not be here. The day will come
when they will grow up and stand by our sides, ready to
start making their own unique contributions to our world.

Physical features aside, the greatest responsibility we
have as parents is to be an inspiration to our children—to
pass on the kind of life that they will strive to imitate. *Have I
been an example of gratitude, hospitality, and courtesy? Have I been
consistent, honest, and hardworking? Was I critical or harsh with my
words, or was I gracious? Did I emphasize the positive traits in
others and promote them to reach their potentials?* These are questions we should ask ourselves. The fact is, our children are

watching, and absorbing, and likely some day will become a reflection of us in more ways than having our chin or nose; they become echoes of our behaviors and attitudes, too.

Education experts agree: Instruction can only go so far. Our children need more than knowledge of good and right things. They need more than good illustrations from literature or history.

The most impactful teaching method is modeling, of showing others the way, rather than merely telling them or pointing them in the right direction. When this modeling example is made by a teacher or a favorite uncle, it can be effective. But when a consistent and worthy example is exhibited by Mom and Dad, something more than an outward resemblance is passed along. Our children might grow up, not only looking like us, but walking and talking like us as well. They will bare our likeness and embody our values, following the standards and principles by which we ourselves have lived in front of them.

The question is not, will we be an example? We are examples! Settle it in your heart right now. Remind yourself: *I have a deep influence on my children.* So the question is, will the example you leave be a good one or a poor one, a light to their path or a shadow to their souls? The choice is yours.

PARENT/CHILD TEAMS

History is replete with stories of successes (and failures) of those who have passed a brightly lit torch to the next generation. Prominent among them in modern history is George H. W. Bush, 41st President of the United States, whose son George W. Bush became the 43rd President, and whose other son Jeb was governor of the state of Florida and was among the leaders of candidates for American President during the 2016 election. In Singapore, Founding Father and Prime Minister Lee Kuan Yew's son Lee Hsien Loong is now the 3rd Chief Executive of the Republic.

Also notable from the world of sports are Bobby and Barry Bonds, a Major League Baseball (MLB) father/son duo who are two of only four players in MLB history to belong to the prestigious 300-300 club (more than 300 home runs and 300 stolen bases). Barry is the all-time home run leader with 762. Steph Curry of the National Basketball Association (NBA), perhaps the best shooter of all time, is the son of Dell Curry, a former NBA star and also father of Steph's younger brother Seth, who also plays for the NBA's Dallas Mavericks.

The same is true in business. The S. C. Johnson & Son, Inc. (thirty-sixth on the Forbes' List)—makers of Windex, Pledge, and Glade—has been run successfully through five generations by Samuel Johnson's descendants since its founding in 1886. The list would not be complete without including the legacy of Sam Walton, founder of Walmart, the world's largest company by revenue as of this writing. Four members of the Walton family are listed in Forbes among the ten richest people in America. What a legacy!

This is not to downplay the influence of mothers or to say that only sons carry on the legacies of their parents. Actor Jon Voight has a famous daughter whose name is now known around the world: Angelina Jolie. Marie Curie, famed female scientist, won two Nobel Prizes (1903 with her husband, and 1911 alone), and was joined by her daughter

Irene in research. Irene went on to earn her own Nobel Prize in Chemistry in 1935 with her husband.

Here is the story of a modern-day father/daughter combo. Rachel writes:

———

Since I was young, I was pretty loud, very "dictatorish," always picking a fight and also very stubborn and headstrong, and you know what? I probably got these genes from my dad. In fact, I remember one person saying to me once, "You are stubborn like your daddy, and it is the very thing that gets you into trouble [with others]."

Yeah, I remember my dad used to "get into all sorts of trouble," too. When he was young, he built a reputation for doing **all the wrong things** (as told to me by Grandma). He got in trouble in school, got in trouble in the army. But as he grew up, he "got in trouble" **for all the right things**.

I remember several years back when there was a highly debated issue in the public scene and my dad "just had to open his mouth" and publicly shared his stand in an interview with BBC radio and the newspaper. It got him into hot water with people who disagreed with him. But at the same time, it won many people's admiration and respect because he was willing to stand up for what is right, to speak out about it, and stick to his guns on it. Whereas, most of us would just hide, not do anything, or at the most make some comments over social media —not Dad.

I am pretty much like my father in this. I may cringe at

first when he does it, but I do the same thing because we're both wired the same way. We'll speak what's on our minds and stand up for what we think is right. Sometimes, I do feel afraid. But when I see my dad, I take courage and stand up for righteousness, and do what a man should be doing instead of hiding behind others. I get courage and am inspired to do the same.

———

Children are predisposed to want to be like us as parents. In the past week, both of my teenage sons have said to me: "Dad, I want to be like you!" I can't imagine a higher honor. I also realize our children's innate desire to be like us is a weighty proposition. The challenge of it motivates us to be the best examples we can be, all the while encouraging them to become solid citizens.

My older children have grown up to pursue careers in medicine, acting, art and design, and social justice. Neither Joyce nor I are in any of these professions, yet we have left our mark on our children in different ways—not so much in the *doing* ways but more in the *being* ways.

There's an old saying that "the apple never falls far from the tree," meaning our children are destined to have many of our traits as parents. I have determined to leave my sons and daughters with a good name, a model for living, a royal consciousness, and a legacy which will one day become an orchard of trees—all bearing good fruit to which many will come and eat and be satisfied. My kids may not think I am the world's fastest or smartest person when they get older. I hope, however, that I will have given them something to be proud of and some things to strive for and emulate. I hope they'll want to be like me.

PUT IT TO WORK

- Gather the family together. **Have each person write down their five most dominant traits.** Then have everyone write down the five most dominant traits of each other. Compare and contrast your findings. Ask each of the children to identify which traits they got from their mother, father, or _____. Note: Umpire the discussion so that it does not move towards pointing out faults or becoming critical. Keep it positive and upbeat!

- **Discuss the meaning of each of your names.** How does the meaning of each name match with the kind of person each one is or is becoming? If you have middle names, do the same with your middle names. If your name is of Northern European origins, you may also be able to find something about the origins of your surname, or even an associated crest. Check out: https://www.heraldryandcrests.com/pages/name-search. If your origins are elsewhere, it would be fun to search for origins and meanings together. Remember, there is something in a name!

- Read the section "The Legacy of Jonathan

Edwards" together. **Dream together about the legacy your family could leave a hundred years from now!** Will people be talking about you as one of those Parent/Child teams who have had a powerful impact on our world?

Chapter Seven

"HEY, YOU'RE REALLY SMART!"

Yesterday is history, tomorrow is a mystery, and today is a gift . . . that's why they call it the present.[31]

— MASTER OOGWAY

O ur eldest daughter, Anna, called. She was a freshman at college, and it was her first semester being away from home. "Dad," she said, "I need some advice." I felt pretty satisfied that she had not gone off to college and forgotten about me! Still, I wasn't fully prepared for the question that followed. "Do you think I should take up ballet or join the rugby team?"

Which page in the parenting manual do you turn to for help in such matters?! Some parents want to be involved in every decision; in fact, some don't only want to be involved, they want to *tell* their children what to do. Other parents are almost never involved, leaving their kids alone to try to navigate without the advantage of their parents' experience and wisdom.

In truth, the role we play in our children's decision making should fall somewhere in between these two extremes. Our goal should be to nurture our children from their youth to be able to make wise decisions for themselves, guiding them to have more and more say as they mature.

We had a good discussion with Anna about which decision was the best fit for her. She had never joined a team sport growing up in Asia, and although we were tentative about it, she decided to join the rugby squad. She thoroughly enjoyed playing for her school's Division I team all four years of university.

GUIDING YOUR CHILDREN TO MAKE DECISIONS

Helping your children to make wise decisions is an indispensable part of our role as parents. Do it well, and you will earn their respect and equip them to be more successful in life.

Here are some guideposts for you to apply as you point your children down successful paths:

- Teach your children the **process** of decision making. Walk them through steps such as having them write down the pros and cons of their decision.

- Discuss with them **practical implications**. If money is borrowed, what does that mean? If a commitment has been made, are they able to fulfill it?

- Ask them to answer the **hard questions**. Are there any moral concerns? Will any values have to be compromised? Any standards lowered?

- Teach them to seek out **wise counsel**. In some cases, that person will not be you but someone else you or your child trusts—someone who has a proven track record.

- Teach your children about **consequences**. No decision should be made without thoroughly examining all the "what ifs" and "what thens."

- Your message should always be, "**I am here** for you," not "Here, let me tell you what to do."

- **Confer with your spouse** first. The bigger the decision, the more necessary it is to involve your spouse in the process, both for confirmation as well as to avoid conflict down the line.

Clearly, we guide our primary school children differently than we do those of our kids in middle school or high school. I find our older children who are married even consult my wife and me before making certain decisions. I believe the reason for this is because they truly benefitted from our guiding them in making wise decisions during the different stages of their lives while they were growing up.

LIFE LESSONS

We learn our most important lessons in life without opening a book, taking a note, or listening to a lecture. Truth is, the most important lessons I learned growing up were from my parents. I learned how to hunt, fish, and ski from my parents—things I have enjoyed all my life. I learned how to change spark plugs, oil, mufflers, and tires from my father. I learned how to do puzzles, sew, make pancakes, and plant a garden from my mother. I learned diligence, sacrifice, and commitment without stepping one foot out of my home or cracking open one book. My grandfather taught me how to play the fiddle, my first instrument, and my father's mother taught me the most important lessons about selfless acts of service.

Children learn so much in life by observation and association. We can go through twelve years of school and never take a class on how to treat guests, strangers, or the elderly. Our high school diploma kept no record of whether we kept our rooms clean and tidy, whether we learned the value of saving money, or whether we learned to love to read. My college degree did not reflect my embracing the values of honesty, generosity, or humility—all things that have contributed greatly to my success in life. I never took a test on how to be a good husband, but a hundred books could not have taught me what I have learned just watching my father interact with my mother over the years.

Now my children are learning "life lessons" from me. I may not have done much to prepare my eldest daughter to be a doctor. But I know she has her list like I do of the many ways that her mother and I have taught her about how to live. The same goes for each of our children. They watch us, and as they do they are acquiring knowledge by the most important means possible: by seeing our example.

So, when I value my wife, when I cherish and praise her, I am teaching my boys how to honor their future wives, and teaching my girls about the kinds of things they should look for in a potential husband. When I prefer their mother or go the extra mile to help out around the house, when I give her a foot rub, tenderly touch her in their presence, or make her a cup of tea in her favorite teacup, the children are "taking a class" that will serve them in their own marriages one day.

Of course, the opposite is also true. If the marriage they observe is one of constant bickering or vying for "rights," or if it is between two bodies that are physically present but are emotionally checked out, their expectations about "marital bliss" will be deeply affected.

DADDY BOSS?

Some cultures and traditions believe that the role of parents is to represent authority and requires preserving a distance between the parents and their children. In companies, the boss always has the biggest office. He sits behind closed doors with a receptionist outside monitoring the times and people who can pass through his "sacred gates." Fathers who try to run their families like this are setting themselves up for a huge disappointment.

Homes should not be run like companies. Children are not our underlings. They can't be employed, and they can't be fired. They should never be made to feel as if they have to align themselves correctly, say the right things, or even perform better than others in order to earn their promotions or gain access to the "boss." *What works around the corporate table does not work around the dinner table.*

While parents deserve respect based upon their position and role, the deepest respect they can gain is not by power but by presence. It's not by title but by time. Not by knowledge but by relationship. Not by lectures but by action.

HARD TOPICS

Being a good example in living a life of integrity before our children is the single most important reason why they will seek us out when they struggle or when they need to talk about one of those "hard" topics. Hard topics require a foundation of trust, and that's not something we can muster on the spot. Trust is earned. It takes time and work to build. Once it is earned, however, difficult topics can be breached so as to ward off disaster. But when trust is shaky, our sons and daughters may well turn to others for advice that can have future-altering consequences.

What am I referring to when I use the term *hard topics*? I'm talking about subjects that children feel uncomfortable talking about with us parents. Sex, for example, is one of those topics. Children are exposed more and more to sex at a younger age. So don't be surprised when they already have more "knowledge" at ten than you did when you were fifteen! Unfortunately, the "experts" in their world are also ten!

Father, you must do whatever it takes to become the "go to guy" for your boy! You must teach him about patience and self-control. Mom, you need to be there for your daughter. She needs to know her worth—that no one else can determine it, neither can another add to or take away from it. You need to let your children know they can come to you when they have questions and when they have struggles.

Teach your children to anticipate a lifetime over which sex is not something shameful or to be feared, but becomes a healthy and wholesome part of life. Teach them about modesty, chastity, and respect. Teach each one about the difference between sex and love.

It may be difficult at first, but as parents we should be initiators. Consider this an axiom: Communication starts with me. If you master the skill of conversation with your children, you will have made it possible to overcome 90 percent of the parenting challenges you will face. If the ties are strong, your words as parents will carry a weight in your children's minds like no other.

My father was of the generation that did not recognize the gravity of influence its words carried. But the things he wrote to me in a letter more than thirty years ago have stayed with me like a tattoo through the years. Others' words are like pencil marks by comparison. But Dad's words, I'll just never forget them.

CURIOSITY

Children are naturally curious. They are born with this insatiable interest in things about which we as adults could care less. While that can be a good thing when they are infants, since they can play with a plastic cover for an hour while Mom gets her housework done, by the time they are two or three, and can start to verbalize their curiosity, parents are all of a sudden faced with a choice: Am I going to answer this question or not?

There comes a time in the life of a young child when his or her fascination with the world demands answers. "Why, Mommy?" "Dad, how did it do that?" "When does that happen?" "Where are we going, today?" At first it can be rather cute, but when the questions come in rapid succession and include a lot of repetition, our patience runs thin. Unlike a vacuum cleaner, a child doesn't come with an on/off switch. It kind of makes us think, *When will they come out with child upgrade, version 2.0, that will correct this obvious design flaw?!*

There is no design flaw here. The problem is not with our three-year-old; it's with us. People learn by doing. Children are born to explore and experiment. A curious child is a healthy child. I should rejoice when she is inquisitive; it is a sign that my child has a gift and potential—that she is eager to learn. When she is encouraged to dig for answers as a child, she will look for solutions when she is an adult. When the thirst for knowledge is aroused during childhood, she will lead an inquisitive life, not for the simple things of youth, but to comprehend the complex ones in an adult world.

My wife and I were by no means perfect in this sense, but *we determined to answer even the most trivial of questions of our children growing up.* The seed of parent/child communication was sown right there when our children were young. We did not want to squelch them because of the inconvenience to us. We tried as best we could to answer meaningfully their curiosity. Looking back, I am glad we did. As our kids have grown, they are now tackling hard questions. They are not intimidated by knotty problems. Seems like curiosity was a blessing in disguise after all.

THE PHONE CHALLENGE

At some point, curiosity is replaced by gadgets. If you have teenagers, most certainly, you have struggled to keep their cell phones out of their hands long enough to have a conversation with them. Cell phones are not just another toy or tool for this generation; they are almost like another body part! So teens naturally think that it is impossible to live without them.

It is wise to set down some rules for phone use, however. How about "no phones during dinner time"? Of course you have to obey your own rule as well! Or how about "no phones after 10 p.m."? You might have to get them an alarm clock so that they don't need their phones through the night. There will be other times when they are overusing their phones. While you might be tempted to confront them or raise your voice about it, try a softer approach. Rather than taking the phone away, use the time to engage them in a discussion about what's important. Or maybe do some reflecting yourself. If your kids are bored, it is possible you have not lit a fire underneath them that makes them live everyday to the fullest.

One thing is sure, your teenager's cell phone does not need to become your enemy! Since your children are undoubtedly using it to connect with their friends and class-mates, why not turn it into an advantage for you? Have you thought about sending messages to them at points throughout the day? A good friend of mine has been sending "words of wisdom" to his children every day for more than five years. They really like it, too, and have even added a lot of their friends to the group! You might not have the time to write something every day, but it means a lot for them to know that you are thinking about them. The phone can actually be a positive tool to build bridges to their hearts.

Something we did was start a family group chat. We post updates about what we are doing and about things that may be of interest to the rest of the family. We may post things about a shared memory, the results of our son's basketball game, or a word of encouragement when someone is facing a challenge or difficulty. We also send pictures and post some fun videos. When many families are being pulled apart by modern technology, we are using it to strengthen our bonds.

All of us will experience some tensions with our children because cell phones have become such an integral part of our lives. But we mustn't see phones as something bad. By setting a few boundaries in place to limit use, and by taking advantage of our phones to stay in regular contact with our family members, they can actually be a great way to stay better connected. In fact, why don't you take a moment to send a sweet note to your spouse right now and then take another sixty seconds to write a text to each of your children, telling them how much you appreciate them. It'll probably be the best use of a few minutes of your time that you will have spent all day.

TEACHING KIDS TO SAVE

We have a tradition at Christmas time. My mother will think of a game we can all play for which a simple reward is given. One year, she filled up a glass jar with quarters, dimes, nickels, and pennies, and the person who guessed the closest to the actual amount that was in the jar received the money as a prize. Our son Daniel guessed right within a few cents, so he won the prize. He was five years old at the time.

Of all our children, Daniel is the one who has the greatest sense about money. He's good at math and has a general fascination with numbers. He also has some creative ways to make money. At one point, he had a "small business" going at school where he would buy individually-wrapped candy in bulk at the market and then sell it to the other students for a slight profit. Business was so good, he even had a couple of other students working for him! One of them was his little sister, who was only six at the time! With the money they earned, they bought a plastic organizer to keep track of every penny.

We believe that kids need to learn responsibility from a young age. They should learn to take care of their own space. They should learn to manage their time well. They should not have to be continually reminded of their homework assignments. And they should learn to be good stewards over their money. When these values are instilled into them from a young age, they will not easily stumble over these matters when they grow up.

Daniel and I have had some good talks about money. I don't want him to become greedy, but I also see in him entrepreneurship and industry that I want to encourage. I have talked with him about the pitfalls and the power we can ascribe to money. I have talked about the joy it can bring when he is able to give it away to help others.

When he got a "job" as a model for a couple of days and received quite a sizable check in the mail, I talked with him about opening a bank account so that he could "grow" his money. His eyes swung open wide. We found a good day when he did not have school and the bank was open, and he carried his money (which was pretty heavy because a lot of it was coins) to open his very first bank account. He was so pleased to find that it was more than one thousand dollars. At the end of the month when the bank statement arrives, we celebrate together the small gains in interest. Hopefully, the lessons and disciplines he is learning now will stay with him over his lifetime.

MINING FOR GOLD

The definition of a prospector is an explorer whose sole purpose is to discover riches under the surface, usually gold. From 1849 to 1855, three hundred thousand people traveled to California from across America and a dozen foreign lands in search of wealth in what later was called *The Gold Rush*. Some struck it rich, but many only faced hardships, leaving debts, debauchery, and broken families in their wake.

A wise parent is like a seasoned prospector. But unlike the temporal and selfish pursuits of these gold diggers, his passion is to explore the riches that lie just beneath the surface of his children, waiting to be brought into the light. Unlike the tens of thousands who suffered greatly and lived with regrets during the great Rush, a parent will never be disappointed if he spends time mining for treasure in his sons and daughters. His investment of time, and sacrifices for a cause, will make discovering bullion seem trivial, even foolish.

Among the prospectors who made millions, many died miserable, disillusioned, or broke, having squandered the wealth for which they had blindly left all else behind. But fathers or mothers who recognize the immense potential in their children—who patiently, skillfully, and prayerfully extract from them gifts, creativity, passions, and talent—have chosen the right priority. They will live to see so much "wealth" created that they will wonder how anyone could have chosen a shiny piece of rock over the enchantment of a child who grows up secure and contented because he knew that, in Mom's and Dad's eyes, he was so much more precious than gold.

NATURALLY CREATIVE

I used to think that some people are creative, and some are not. Now, I realize that in fact we all have the capacity and potential to be creative but in different ways. I understand, for instance, that I have my creative side even if I am not good at drawing. I easily see connections and relationships between words, I enjoy writing, I have done some songwriting, and I even have choreographed and won a dance contest.

Joyce is artistic in totally different ways. She has a natural ability to see compatible colors and match shapes and things of different sizes, gifts that make her a natural interior designer. I have enjoyed seeing the world through her eyes even as I appreciate her innate gifts.

One of the most important things I can do as a parent is to guide my children in discovering their creative sides. Therefore, Joyce and I have always looked for ways to unleash the "right brain"[32] potential of our children. We praise their "works of art" even though they may not appear prodigious at first. We don't have a TV subscription but rather encourage them to read, play games, build things, do projects, or learn a skill, hobby, or sport during their free time. The results have been astounding. In this environment, they effortlessly and spontaneously generate ideas and never seem to tire of learning.

Here are several things we have learned that may help you to let the flowers of innovation blossom in your children:

- **Acknowledge** that we are all creative in our own way. Start looking at your sons or daughters and say to yourself: *He has a huge potential to create. She has a gift of imagination. It's my job to nurture their gifts.*

- **Encourage** exploration. Let your kids draw, even

it if begins with tracing or rubbings. Some may draw better or will be better working with their hands while others will be the designer types or be musically inclined.

- **Celebrate** their work. Rembrandt was not born in a day. Post their drawings, display their Lego creations, and give them awards and praise for a job well done.

- **Commit** to development. Once you discover a natural gift, help your son or daughter become more skillful, set aside time for practice, or find a class, teacher, or mentor to hone these skills to perfection.

- **Generate** momentum. You may not have seven kids, but one of the dynamics at work in our household is that the children feed off each other's gifts and readily learn from each other. The same could be achieved by inviting some of your children's friends to your house to do these kinds of things together, or by sending them to a camp where peers with similar interests are striving to develop their talents.

- **Reduce** rivalries. Our experience is that TV and computer time needs to be monitored and restricted greatly. Some shows or games can enhance creativity when done in a balanced and guided way. But their use should be limited in

order to allow for a rich imagination to be
cultivated.

Unleashing your creative side can be an exhilarating and
lifetime pursuit. Nurturing these gifts and skills in your
children can also be one of the most rewarding aspects of
your role as a parent. One of our daughters is a professional
actress. Our oldest son has sold a number of paintings for
hundreds of dollars. Your kids may not only unearth some
sources of joy and passion that will stay with them for a lifetime in the process; they may also think you are pretty cool
(even smart!) for doing so.

A FOUNTAIN OF WISDOM

The man who is most famous in history for writing proverbs
has a proverbial phrase that refers to him: "wise as
Solomon." This oft-used idiom is a testament to a man
whose name has become synonymous with wisdom.

Solomon was rich. Solomon was powerful. But there was
nothing as daunting about Solomon as his wisdom. World
leaders would travel great distances, bearing gifts, to pay
him homage, to marvel at his wealth, to seek opportunities
for trade, or to form alliances with him. They were struck by
the grandeur of his palace and spellbound by the order and
discipline of his administration and staff. But of all these
things, it was the fact of his ability to answer every question
that they had with astuteness and acumen which left them
with, as said by the Queen of Sheba, "no more spirit," in
them.[33]

So where did Solomon get all this wisdom? Through

his writings we know, and it could not have been said more emphatically: *from his father and mother.* Three thousand proverbs and more than one thousand songs are attributed to Solomon. Somehow he managed to find the time to write all these while he was busy ruling one of the world's largest kingdoms in his day. And time and time again, he gave credit where credit was due. Twenty-two times in the book of Proverbs he specifically credits his father David for imparting the lofty nuggets of insight to him. That means, while King David was ruling his empire, he was taking the time to instruct, train, and admonish his son, causing Solomon to pen many such words as these:

> *My son, keep your **father's** command,*
> *And do not forsake your **mother's** teaching.*
> *Bind them always on your heart;*
> *fasten them around your neck.*
> *When you walk, they will guide you;*
> *When you sleep, they will watch over you;*
> *When you wake up, they will speak to you.*
> *For a command is a lamp, this teaching is a light,*
> *And correction and instruction are the way to life.*[34]

Simply put, fathers and mothers are a great source of wisdom. But like David, fathers need to take the time to share their experiences and valuable lessons they have learned in the school of life with their sons and daughters. And like Solomon, children should consider their parents' Ivy League potential as a resource on how to face challenges, solve difficulties, and circumvent defeat.

Francine from Manila was thirteen when she made this invaluable discovery about her parents:

———

When I was thirteen, my parents sent me to a study tour in Taiwan. For the year prior to this tour, I was adamant about not wanting to go because I thought that it was going to be boring—with my precious summer days spent in Mandarin classes. However, after some, actually a lot, of convincing and guidance from my parents, I finally decided to go on this study tour.

Accompanied by several of my fellow students and a few teachers, I left the country without my parents for the first time in my life. For the whole three weeks of the tour, I was responsible for everything that my parents would normally be responsible for, and this was the time of my life when I started appreciating all those household chores and life lessons that I—sometimes happily, sometimes grudgingly—followed. I had to budget my expenses, do my own laundry, wash the dishes, cook food, and account for all my belongings. Being able to apply those life lessons that my parents taught me certainly made me become more independent, a skill that I continue to appreciate and employ every day as an elder sister to four younger siblings.

One of the hardest yet valuable lessons I learned was how to socialize. Throughout all the activities, I had no access to Wi-Fi, meaning that I had to put away my phone and talk to people. Given that the people around me were schoolmates, one would have thought that I was already close with them. However, I was an introverted, shy child who got anxious every time I talked to someone who was not a family member or a close friend. Having to put the phone away really forced me to develop tight bonds and relationships with my fellow tour-mates. I now find it so much easier to make friends!

Halfway through the trip, I realized that my preconceptions on what I would be doing on the trip were way off. Learning Mandarin, which was important but slightly mind-numbing, was only a microscopic aspect of the trip compared to all the other activities I was able to participate in. Over the course of the trip, I was able to learn about Taiwanese culture and history, go hiking and camping, participate in team-building and leadership activities, go on excursions, and learn new sports. I realized that I had been too close-minded and immediately assumed that I would not enjoy the trip while my parents knew, on the other hand, that it would suit me perfectly.

At the end of the tour, I was crying, begging them to let me stay a wee bit longer. I really enjoyed the tour so much, but if it had not been for my parents' encouragement, I would not even have gone on my own volition. Experience just makes parents know what's best for us children even if we might not realize or appreciate it at the time. However, now that I've grown and looked back on this once-in-a-lifetime experience, I really don't know how I could ever repay them. This trip taught me my parents are, well, really smart!

———

KUNG FU OOGWAY

Kung Fu Panda is one of the most successful animated movies ever produced. With an all-star voiceover cast, *Panda* is a parody of a Chinese martial arts film where a bumbling, overweight, and over-hungry panda (named Po) with no training is chosen by the kingdom's wisest resident, Oogway, to take on the evil and deadly Tai Lung, a snow leopard. Less skilled than others, virtually untrained, physically totally unfit, the hopes of the entire kingdom are placed on the overmatched Po to defeat powerful Tai Lung.[35]

So what is the lesson here? Po does not win by physical prowess or advanced techniques. He wins because the smartest person in the kingdom saw something in him that nobody else saw. The old tortoise "Oogway," the most famous Kung Fu master in Chinese history, clearly was not putting anyone away with his lightning speed.

Though strangely downplayed in our day, *Panda* shows us there *is* great value in heeding the voice of the ancients. It was Oogway's age which was his greatest asset, harnessing all the years of accumulated wisdom into the most formidable weapon. In that sense, Master Tortoise has a great lesson to teach us as well: We are vulnerable, doing ourselves a great disservice, when we ignore the true masters in our lives.

CONCLUSION

Unfortunately, Oogway is an anomaly among modern-day entertainment, education, and art. Not many Jedis were lining up to learn from Obi-wan Kenobi.[36] And despite the powers and wizardry of Gandalf, not many hobbits, or anyone else for that matter, were following closely in the footsteps of this sage.[37] The setting of Kung Fu Panda is *not* modern-day China, where once-held practices of deep regard for the elderly have largely gone with the wind. Google and FaceBook are a much more natural source of guidance to us in the twenty-first century. Why do I have to go over the river and through the woods to Grandmother's house?

Solomon's own son rejected his teachings. Rehoboam had direct access to all the great proverbs and the countless, precious, hours spent with his own father growing up. Upon ascendancy to the throne, the counsel of Solomon's cabinet of judicious, experienced, compassionate leaders were at his command. Instead, he turned to the young men who were his peers for advise on how to rule. The foolish decisions he made as a result divided and weakened the powerful nation of Israel into two rival kingdoms, a condition from which it never recovered.

It is not easy to be a respected old master these days. Even the wisest rulers find it difficult to pass all their wisdom on to their own sons and daughters. But by a combination of skill and technique, through patience and practical means, we as parents can become a fountain of wisdom to our children.

We need to build the bridges of communication, mine the treasures of their gifts and interests, teach them the practical things of how to live, how to save, and how to make good decisions. Beginning at their beginnings, be a resource to them, then live the kind of life that engenders their trust and enchants them to follow. Your kid doesn't have to think you are old and irrelevant. Hey, he or she might even grow up thinking, *You're really smart!*

PUT IT TO WORK

- If you know that your children are facing a decision, don't wait for them to come to you for help. They might assume you are not interested and find someone else who is! **Follow the list from the section "Guiding Your Children to Make Decisions."** Bring along a piece of paper and make two columns, pros and cons. Share a personal experience you had with the subject, or maybe engage your spouse in that part of the conversation if he or she has more experience in that area than you do. Resist the temptation to just provide answers. Even though you think you know what is best, you will have performed a far greater service in training them in the process of making decisions than in making the decision for them.

- **Take some time to talk about the "hard topics."** Good communication with your children is one of your greatest assets as you journey along the path of parenting.

- **Set some guidelines for your phones and gadgets** (make sure you follow your own rules when it applies!). Then if you don't have one yet,

set up a family chat group and watch the
fun begin!

- **Follow the steps in the "Naturally Creative"
  section,** and start letting the flowers of
  innovation bloom in your children.

- If you have not already done so, **help your kids**
  (at the age appropriate time) **to start their own
  savings account!**

Chapter Eight

"OLD-FASHIONED AIN'T SO BAD"

Good, old-fashioned ways keep hearts sweet, heads sane, hands busy.[38]

— LOUISA MAY ALCOTT

*E*ach generation feels like it is better than the one before it. Computers are faster, transportation is easier, TV screens are bigger and have sharper images, and athletes keep breaking the records of those who have preceded them. To many, old things are in danger or being discarded on the scrap heap of irrelevance. But children who discover the gems of traditions have stumbled upon an oft hidden treasure. They may discover that playing board games with friends is more satisfying than playing a computer game by themselves, or that a thousand "friends" on Facebook are not as precious as one or two good ones with whom they can share their hearts and lives. They might even discover that the things Mom and Dad used to do for entertainment really are a whole lot of fun!

My fascination with history dates back to the treasure I own in some of my earliest memories. Our family rented an upstairs apartment from an elderly couple, Charlie and Mamie. I remember occasionally venturing down to their house for a tall glass of milk and some homemade cookies, but the thing that stands out more than anything else was sitting on Charlie's knee and listening to him tell stories. It's one thing to watch a TV series about Davy Crockett, an American folk hero from the early 1800s, or read about the adventures of Huckleberry Finn from a slightly later period. Charlie was living history! He told tall tales of crossing the Midwest in a covered wagon and of meeting real, live, Native Indian tribes. So olden days were never wrapped in a dull, drab cloak for me. They were like a coat of many colors. A part of me has always wondered why everyone doesn't feel the same!

HUMAN LIGHTHOUSES

People have not only lost touch with their traditions, many have also lost their appreciation for them. Not so many years ago (indeed, there are even some of these places left in remote pockets of the planet), people received most of their values and perspectives through the eyes of their elderly. They were the keepers of the stories and the custodians of those things about which our families harnessed pride. Their words were given full attention at family gatherings, even as they were allotted the finest seats. Their wisdom had been achieved through rich experiences accumulated over a lifetime, serving to both warn us not to make the same mistakes they may have made while, at the same time, inviting us to stand upon their shoulders in facing our own challenges. If we do not embrace the benefits of these ancestral lighthouses, we may well find ourselves floundering in treacherous waters in the dark. By neglecting them, we may be lifting the anchors meant to stabilize us only to be left adrift, subject to the vicissitudes of cultural winds and social waves.

I was raised in New England where lighthouses have dotted the Northeast American coastline for hundreds of years. They warn of dangerous shoals and reefs, and guide vessels large and small to safely enter harbors and ports. I did not realize it at the time, but I had a well-lit path due to the beacons coming from the human landmarks in my own life. We frequently spent time with our grandparents on both sides of my family. In fact, both sets of my grandparents were neighbors and good friends with each other! Sometimes, we stayed with them; sometimes, they stayed with us. Looking back, I now realize they resembled lighthouses in another very tangible way: They were totally free. Ships never had to pay for the services of the lighthouse, and no one has to pay a penny for the beams streaming from those in our family who have blazed many a winding trail ahead of us.

I learned contentment from my mother's parents. They had ten kids and yet lived in a small house that had a constant stream of traffic running through it. Amazingly, they always had enough food to go around. Both of my mother's parents had a contagious humor which makes me smile on every thought of them. Evenings were spent in hymn-filled bliss as Grammy tickled the piano keys and Grandpa sawed the bow of one of his many well-warn violins.

From my father's mother, I learned diligence and simplicity. Much of her life, she lived out of a suitcase, ever ready in the trunk of her car. A retired nurse, in the days before home health and hospice care were popular, she self-lessly served family and friends who had fallen ill, staying as long as she was needed. I will never forget her baking forty pies for our family in a single day (from apples which she personally picked and peeled), before she headed south to warmer weather for the winter. My paternal grandfather died when I was pretty young, but he was a gentle giant in my eyes, a man of stature who probably never had an ill thought for anyone in his lifetime.

THROWING AWAY OUR ELDERLY

Sadly, many people's attitudes towards our elderly have "gone south," too. A man from the island of Fiji, which maintains a rich tradition of care and respect for their elderly, commented to anthropologist Jared Diamond, "You [the West] throw away your old people."

Yikes! The statistics support the Fijian's harsh words. In the U.S. alone, more than half a million reports of abuse against elderly Americans reach authorities every year, and millions more cases go unreported. These include abandonment, financial exploitation, and physical, emotional, or sexual abuse. True, these are the extreme cases. Many elderly are just left in nursing homes and go weeks on end without so much as a peep from their children. In one case, an 82-year-old woman's death was determined to be homicide by neglect. The last six months of her life, though she lived with two of her adult relatives, were spent with her sitting affixed to a chair in her bedroom.

Even the cultures steeped in traditions of "filial piety" have not escaped the flood of disregard for the elderly that has swept the world in the wake of urbanization. Perhaps nowhere has this been more pronounced than in China. The massive migration of people to look for work and prosperity in the cities means millions and millions of parents have been left uncared for in the villages. Below is an example reported by the Associated Press on July 1, 2013:

> Although respect for the elderly is deeply ingrained in Chinese society, three decades of market reforms have accelerated the breakup of China's traditional extended family, and there are few affordable alternatives, such as retirement homes. News outlets frequently carry stories about elderly parents being abused or neglected, or of children seeking to take control of their parents' assets without their knowledge. State media reported this month that a grandmother in her 90s in the prosperous eastern province of Jiangsu had been forced by her son to live in a pig pen for two years.[39]

It is not only village dwellers who have been cast aside either. The plethora of high-profile cases from China's major cities formed a crescendo to which the Chinese government responded by instituting the "Elderly Rights Law." It warns adult children to "never neglect or snub elderly people." The law is Beijing's attempt to stem this tide by introducing punishments of fines, even jail time, for offenders.

ANCESTRY.COM

A high school social studies assignment proved to be another milestone for me in my connection with my past. Members of my class were asked to produce individual "family trees." What started as a relatively simple task ended up becoming a formidable project that absorbed my attention for many months to come.

I interviewed family members and frequented the local historical societies. I went to remote cemeteries to uncover the names, births, and inscriptions of my ancestors. What I found often pointed to other family members who were buried nearby. I plowed through old church records and chatted with town clerks, while running into others who had a shared passion about the history of Vermont where my family has lived for nine generations.

I visited old homesteads. My spirit often was carried to the days in which my ancestors lived with vivid wonderment, if not a bit of fantasy. From the information I had gathered, I recognized some of their characteristics in myself or my siblings. I relived their journeys, their successes, their losses. A pond had been named after our family here and a street there. They had been among the original five families who had settled in and chartered a town which is only five miles from where my parents live today. And in an amazing twist of fate, my son-in-law, whose family now lives twelve thousand miles from mine, has ancestors in my state going back to the 1700s, and after some research we discovered his relatives are friends and neighbors of my parents!

I have made a solid determination that my children will not be extracted from their roots and will not be unmoored from their past like anchors cut off to sink into the mire of a distant past never to be recovered again. This is easier said than done.

Many have imbibed a lie that the past is boring or that the people who lived in former times were ignorant. It's sad that such lies can keep us from connecting to the true brilliance, stick-to-itiveness, determination, and work of generations before us. Their lives accomplished so many things that we enjoy, use, or depend upon today.

Sometimes, when I hear people say they're bored studying history or they don't think much of the older generation, I'm tempted to think, *You think you're so smart with your "smart phones" and gadgets. Who do you think produced the science and technology that gave you those things? It was an older generation!*

Indeed, I've wondered if our "smart phones" are helping to raise a generation of dummies. We used to have to learn how to spell; now our computers do it for us. People used to use their brains to calculate; now everything from calculators to cash registers do it for them. Last week when riding on the subway, I told my son to look around. Every person was absorbed by their phones or their iPads; most were playing mindless games. I told him it was not that long ago that people had conversations with the people around them as they all traveled together to work. What a novel idea!

Last year, I spent six months reading *The Little House on the Prairie* to my youngest children, ages seven, ten, and twelve. There are nine books in the popular series. These tell of the real life experiences of a pioneering family on the American western frontier during the late 1800s. We talked about our reading during the day, and everyone looked forward to that sacred time when we could sit down to explore right alongside these brave pioneers.

My children learned to appreciate history during our reading together. They were constantly reminded how blessed they are with all their modern-day conveniences and comforts. They asked questions and learned new vocabulary, and their imaginations were stimulated in ways that were, frankly, inspirational. Let me tell you what I mean.

The power of imagination is hugely important but is threatened by the onslaught of social media and gaming in our day. Though it is a blessing to have movies and video images in our generation, the tradeoff is that the world of the imagination is often underutilized if not left dormant. One of the great benefits of listening to a story is you play the story in your brain rather than "lazily" watching it on a screen.

This was really brought home to me when I was reading the fifth book and a man returned to the scene—a man whom we had met back in the second book. Before the author had indicated who he was by name, the children already knew who he was because, as they explained to me, they could "see" him. I was amazed. A discussion followed that helped me to realize that, the whole time I was reading, they were not simply and passively listening. They were mentally engaged. They were creating the scenes and the images of people described in the story, making their own mental "movie" as I read.

RAISING CLASSICAL CHILDREN

My children like to listen to classical music during the twenty-minute ride to school in the morning. Even our seven-year-old said the other day that she recognized one of the pieces that was playing as being from a cartoon she had watched. When the next piece came on, which was the background for a movie with high drama, I asked her to describe what kinds of emotions were being depicted by the different styles of music as they ebbed and flowed. Her answers were astute.

Why shouldn't children of this generation learn to appreciate these amazing works of art? After all, they are the result of such genius, truly credits to the heights of creativity and prowess that are uniquely human. With up to ninety musicians in an orchestra, all playing their instruments with their variations of sounds and mood, and yet made to harmonize and move in and out, up and down in resplendent glory, what's not to appreciate? When we consider that the universally recognized greatest composers of all time lived two to three hundred years ago, it should be a wakeup call to those who dismiss old things as cobwebbed relics not worthy of time and attention.

My son Jeremy (15) writes of his appreciation for "old-fashioned" things here:

"Jawolh herr kommandant!" Perhaps not very many of my peers have any idea what this means, or have even heard of *Hogan's Heroes* (1965–1971), the American TV sitcom from

which the line came. But then, there are many who have not heard of Abbott and Costello or seen the Marx Brothers movie *Duck Soup* either. So I consider it quite special that I have had a whole magical world of some of the finest traditions in entertainment and culture that have been a part of my upbringing.

I love to watch Fred Astaire dance on the walls and ceiling, and scenes from *Singing in the Rain, Annie,* or *The Music Man* often come to mind. And it is not just the "If I Were A Rich Man" of film (a song from *The Fiddler on the Roof)*, we've also interacted with history through the nine-book series, *The Little House on the Prairie,* chronicling the lives of early American pioneers.

My dad loves to read to us. Not only has he read the *Little House* books, but he has read biographies of interesting people who lived a hundred or more years ago. We've visited historical sites in China and Europe, and enjoy museums wherever we go. It's all such an important part of our family lifestyle.

All this has created a love for all things old in me. I am fascinated by old cars. I have a collection of old toys. When I sit down at the piano, I love to play hymns or songs from eras gone by. From the time I was small, I have always been an inquisitive kid. My parents said I asked questions non-stop! I'm so thankful that my parents have stirred my imagination in all these ways.

I remember when I was eight our family visited Williamsburg, Virginia. Seeing what it was like to live in a colonial village was just so cool to me! I remember the harpsichord, the old carpenter's workshop, and the triangular hats. At the time, it seemed like the things themselves were what was awesome. It was only years later that I realized that was not the case.

A hat is just a hat, no matter what shape it is in. There is nothing so special about a hat, that's a fact! But what is special is that hat had a history. Someone was inspired to design three-cornered hats that became so popular all the men and boys were wearing them. The hats—like the rope-makers, the blacksmiths, and the cabinet makers—were all windows through which we could see a world of how people lived three hundred years ago. Wow!

I will never forget how my dad and mom have exposed me to the past. I so appreciate them sitting down together with us to watch those old shows. I once heard it said that history isn't history without a story. The *Mona Lisa* would just be another painting if it weren't for the story behind it. Someday, two hundred years from now, who knows, maybe someone will know me through my story, too!

———

My fling with the past does not make me a traditionalist, toting a banner that exalts all things ancient, while being critical of all things new. Quite the contrary, I am not the least bit interested in impeding progress. I do not reject the new when I encourage my family to embrace things deemed old-fashioned. While there is a natural tension between the two, we must consider that gravity actually helps a plane to fly. In the same way that rejecting gravity will keep a plane grounded, so rejecting the past will also prevent us from soaring as we are meant to.

Jesus spoke about a wise master bringing out of his

storehouse "new treasures as well as old." Although the quote "those who cannot remember the past are condemned to repeat it" was written by George Santayana, it are more famously remembered spoken by a bombastic Winston Churchill. It is profitable to reach into the past without living in the past. It is wise to walk in the ways that have been well trodden, even as we blaze new paths for ourselves and posterity. History may appear boring to some, but to those who have discovered its richness, it can become a cherished and bosom friend.

VINTAGE

Contemporary British author Fennel Hudson masterfully strokes these sentiments in his writing:

> Mine is a so-called vintage existence, anachronistic living, made all the more rewarding by keeping a raised eyebrow on the absurdities of modern life.[40]

Mr. Hudson captures something here. What is a "vintage existence"? The word *vintage* invokes images of something classy, stylish, or excellent. Broken and marred things are not referred to as vintage; rather, things that have increased in value over time, befitting people of stature, these are vintage. Only things or people worthy of honor bear this distinction.

When I was young, my home region had an annual antique car show where majestic, rare, dinosauric vehicles would stop people in their tracks to echoes of oohs and aahs. Polished and crisp, people came from virtually every state, wooed by the mystique of these four-wheeled ambassadors of the glorious days of old.

My grandfather kept a 1940 Buick that I even got to ride in during the Fourth of July parade one year. I still remember feeling so proud perched in this sleek, buffed symbol of the "good ol' days."

My sense is it was not just the artistic or unique nature of these vehicles that was kindling our fascination. There is simply something magical about those days when life was simpler and slower: a time when a car was not driven but "taken out for a ride." In those days, a girl was "courted" by quiet walks and nights spent on the porch swing rather than swept away to gut-pounding music backdropped by strobe lights.

Vintage speaks of wines that have been bottled with motherly care from the best grapes, of the best years, by the best wineries, kept for the finest hour, an occasion befitting a signature and crowning moment. The lifted goblet, the gentle *cling* of the toast, a *swish*, a *whiff*, and then only one mouthful of the fruits of years of exquisite aging in ancient oaken barrels passed down from generations—such pomp and ceremony speak of the worth of treasure in each bottle. That is vintage. That is fashion corked in something old.

History does not record the mundane so much as it does

these signposts of achievement, the events worthy of our commemoration. Young people are prone to gaze ahead, for they have no history, no roots, no starting point on their GPS unless we give these things to them. We must stop and consider the quality of the foundation we are giving them. The parents who fail to anchor their children in healthy traditions risk lifting the kite while cutting the string. Will we serve them a powdered drink whipped up in an instant, or pour them a crystal wineglass full of a rare chardonnay from the wine cellar of a rich heritage? This is our choice.

THE TREASURE OF TRADITIONS

My penchant for traditions arises from yet another important discovery: The values upon which healthy families are built are promoted or maintained by most of the older stories, movies, and memories of yesteryear. Since I am singularly committed to establishing the strongest possible foundation for my family, injecting every means at my disposal which lends itself to success, why would I wink at this verdant provision? Why would I subject my children to the unbridled screening of infidelity when I want to breed faithfulness? Why expose them to promiscuity, violence, foul language, or acrid humor when my vision for them is that they might be honorable, peace-loving, and an encouragement to the people who are around them?

The media that bombards them every day taps the sensational because it sells. I would rather risk being called *old-fashioned* and watch a Shirley Temple movie. You may think it will never work, but it has for me. Laurel and Hardy may have been immortalized long ago, but they are still very much alive in our household, at my sons' and daughters' behest.

So how does a family draw from the wealth of this account? Here are some suggestions:

- Speak of some of your own positive and beneficial takeaways from the past. Talk about not only your insights but include those of your parents, ancestors, nation, etc.

- Allow grandparents or family members from the older generation to mix with your children, and create the context whereby some of the great stories can be passed down.

- Intersperse your movie selections with some of the classics (e.g. *Wizard of Oz, Mary Poppins,* etc.)

- Do the same with some old TV series. *I Love Lucy* is sure to be a winner!

- Reading a book or series like *The Little House on the Prairie* worked very well for us. This or another similar book that chronicles wholesome family values would be a great place to start.

- Visit some awesome museums together. Then spend some time talking about the experiences. Antique stores are also a rich source for stirring the imaginations of your children.

- Work on some projects together that help to link your children with their past, such as constructing a family tree, organizing and storing old photographs, or making a scrapbook.

- Organize a family reunion or take advantage of an existing holiday or festival during which extended family will be present, and plan events that are fun, commemorating some of the ancient treasures that are uniquely a part of your family's identity.

I've shed a few tears as I have walked down memory lane writing this chapter. I see my grandfather doing a handstand on the roof of his little house after he and uncles and friends had completed it. I see his chin resting on the fiddle that he often took to the local nursing homes to cheer up the old folks who were there. I feel the tickle of the stubbled finger of my other grandfather reaching around or under his rocking chair as I tried to hide from him. I recall the fun-filled nights of playing dominoes or cards, or doing a puzzle with my father's mom.

My mother's mom also had an old car, a '56 Studebaker, but she had a lap so inviting yet I was too big to sit on. We could only cuddle around her as she kept us all a-laughing with her jokes and cheery disposition. When she finally "went on to her reward," she had no less than 166 living descendants and what seemed like half the town present at her funeral at the Methodist Church in the town's center.

I know that we, or our children, may face a certain amount of ridicule for our passion for the past. Riding the current like those who are rushing towards a seemingly more exciting future is effortless and popular. But for me and my house, we are going to risk it. Like the mighty salmon, we choose to swim against the current to reach the upper, narrower channels of the stream where the spawning of life takes place. We may be bucking trends, but we do so with confidence that we are uncovering a vast trove of treasure. Old-fashioned ain't so bad after all.

PUT IT TO WORK

- **Find creative and positive ways to connect your children with their grandparents** and others among the elderly in your and your spouse's families. Ask them to tell some of their favorite stories! If they have passed on, or are very far away, make friends with some interesting elderly people near you. Family is best, but some would be happy to "adopt" you if you are willing to "adopt" them!

- **Study your family tree.** Make it a family project. If you do have elderly from your family, get them involved, too!

- Our kids learned to love history through reading *The Little House on the Prairie* together. **If you have not read to your kids in a long time, start with one book**, and maybe bring it as a way of spicing up a vacation by reading together for twenty minutes each night.

- Taking our kids to Williamsburg was probably one of the best ideas we ever had to nurture an appreciation for things from the past. If Williamsburg is too far for you, **find something nearer which allows your children to see the way people used to live**, and even get some hands-on experience with ancient ways.

- There are a number of other suggestions in the "Treasure of Traditions" section. **Rent a Shirley Temple movie**, or *Mary Poppins,* and watch it together. Have fun!

Chapter Nine

"CAN WE BE FRIENDS?"

Romance fails us and so do friendships, but the relationship of parent and child, less noisy than all the others, remains indelible and indestructible, the strongest relationship on earth.[41]

— THEODOR REIK

When I was young, I had platform shoes, wore bell-bottom pants, grew my hair long, and would say things were groovy and out o' sight when I really liked them. That was around the same time that my parents purchased our first color TV set, on which we could watch channels three, five, four (which was called channel twenty-two, but I never figured out why!), and eight. Channels twelve and six were in and out. Sometimes it looked like the shows were filmed in a blizzard!

Times have changed. The length of our hair or the kind

of TV we watch are surface issues. The way that we relate to each other as times change affects us to the core. When I was young, it never occurred to me that I could be "friends" with my mom, or especially my dad. He was "up there," and I was "down here." My three brothers and I never dared to talk back to our father. He never really sat down and had a heart-to-heart conversation with me or my brothers. We never expected it, and therefore we were not disappointed when it didn't happen!

I was never afraid of my dad, for I knew him to be kind and gentle, but you could say that I feared him. He seemed large, just not in the physical sense. When he spoke, his words were weighty, so that I never questioned him. It would have been unnatural, like a soldier in basic training talking back to his sergeant. It was not like he was never wrong; it was that his being wrong would still have been better than my insisting on being right. It's just the stature dads held in our eyes back then was higher, and my dad lived up to every inch of it. In fact, he was an amazing dad!

If you try to raise your kids today the way you were raised, you will fail them. As sure as people are not listening to Diana Ross and the Bee Gees on the radio these days, kids are not going to be satisfied with your being a distant figurehead and dispenser of words that must be heeded "no matter what." Those were superlative days when people said things like, "Your father knows *best!*" "Don't you *ever* talk back to me!" "Do it now, *no* questions asked!" Not anymore. Nowadays, it's not unusual to hear kids say: "I don't think so, Dad." "You're wrong, Mom. I checked it out on Google." "Hey, guys, I got this!" The shift in perspective and family culture has been nothing short of seismic.

THE GENERATION GAP

It's imperative that we adapt to this shift. The chasm between generations has been broadly affected by the sheer pace of change that is whizzing past us in this technological and media revolution. The sooner we realize it and make the necessary adjustments, the better. Ignoring change does not make it go away. As we face it head-on, we are likely to discover it's not necessarily a bad thing either!

Although challenge of closing the gap is intimidating, I've learned that there are a lot of positives in the new paradigm for the parent/child relationship. The most I could have hoped for in my generation was to have some mutual interests with my parents, to share some laughs, and to keep the peace. The formal nature of things in those days meant things were "comfortable." Because we knew our place as kids, the boundaries were much clearer, creating the impression of a "safe distance." Friendship, however, was out of the question.

With the "Yes, Sir" of yesteryear fading, with boundary lines being wiped away, a new casual flair has paved the way for a different kind of bond between parents and their children. Our suits and blouses have been replaced by T-shirts and jeans. Loafers and high heels have given way to Nikes and sandals.

The new parenting paradigm means there is now the possibility that kids sit *with* their parents, and not just *next to* them; it means we don't talk *at* each other, but we speak *to* each other. It means conversation is not solely about information sharing but intention. It means, if we as parents win their hearts, we are not simply seen as successful in their eyes but awesome! It means we have moved past being honored to being admired. It means we can become their friends.

DATING YOUR KIDS

Joyce and I have unearthed a most enjoyable and efficient way to fan the flame of friendship with our kids: Date them. Ask our daughters what a DDD or an MDD is, and you are sure to get a shy, warm response. Daddy/Daughter and Mommy/Daughter Dates are an important part of our family culture. I don't know who looks forward to them more, us or them! If you aren't doing this with your kids, it's time to start.

The DDD/MDD does not have to be something extraordinary. We do the same with our sons, too. You don't have to spend a lot of money, and you don't have to go to the local theme park to have a meaningful time with one of your children. Joyce and I have learned that just being together, one on one, even doing things that we do routinely, can be special. The point is not *what* you do, or *where* you do it, but that you as a parent are making precious time to specifically and personally spend with each of your children.

We may think that our children mean a lot to us. We may tell other people how much we care about our children. We may even tell our own children (yes!) that we are proud of them or praise them for their creativity and hard work. But love is a four-letter word, and it is spelled T-I-M-E. There is simply no substitute for spending quality time with our sons and daughters.

Let them choose where you are going to eat. Buy a small memento. Take some "selfies." Ask them how things have been going lately. Talk about what's been happening in school or in their friendships. You will likely find as we have that in these times our sons or daughters open up about some personal struggles. You may make an important discovery about how he or she thinks, or about some gift, talent, or interest he or she might have. You can share something about yourself that you might not typically talk about with more people around. All healthy relationships are give and take, not just giving, and not just taking.

If you have never dated your kids, why not plan your first one today? If you think you don't have enough time to ever do this, then you could very likely have to spend even more (negative) time in the future correcting painful situations that result from your myopic choice. What could have been a positive interaction can evolve into an embarrassing or problematic one. I have seven children and have managed to set aside date time with all of them. You can, too.

BRIDGES

The need to be proactive in building bonds and closing gaps with our children is beautifully illustrated by a village I once visited. It faced a unique and troubling dilemma. For hundreds of years, this village benefitted from its location on the bank of a major river. Its goods were traded by the boat traffic. The villagers served traders and travelers and could travel easily themselves. There was an abundance of fish. As civilization grew up around the village, the river became redundant. As other cities had sprung up on the other side of the river, the villagers discovered they were inauspiciously situated on the proverbial wrong side.

Not large or influential enough to attract interest in the large investment needed to build a bridge, they resigned themselves to the inconvenience of traveling long distances to get to the nearest bridge, or to cross the river by boats that had long fallen into disrepair. One day, a boat capsized. Villagers died.

The principal of the school and a small church got together and decided to turn tragedy into opportunity. A committee was formed. Funds were raised. A team of people covenanted together to give of their time and talents. After months of planning, construction began, bringing old and young, male and female, and rich and poor together to build a bridge. The effort itself brought healing, and although the bridge will never dawn the covers of travel magazines, it restored hope to this once vibrant village.

This story serves as a powerful lesson for us as parents. We don't have to live with gaps between us and our sons and daughters. And God forbid that we wait for tragedy to strike before we commit ourselves to action. It may be costly and seemingly insurmountable at first, but once we decide to build bridges, the healing begins. Hope is restored. Before our very eyes, the gap that once brought untold frustration disappears as the bridge performs its magic.

Commit yourself to building bridges to and with your kids. The rewards are for a lifetime, and beyond.

FINDING COMMON GROUND

One of the best ways to ford the river that divides is to take practical steps to understand and appreciate your children's interests. It doesn't mean you have to go with them to a Justin Bieber concert! But it does mean that you explore the realm of their likes and dislikes, and mine for the treasures of talents and special gifts they possess.

Once you find them, they will be more precious than gold to you. Harness your discoveries by nurturing the things you find. Once you touch the very core of who they are, their estimation of you transforms. You will have gained access to their hearts.

Next, find things that you can do together. A friend and colleague of mine came up with a very creative idea. During a time of soul-searching for ways to strengthen the bonds of his family, as he was enrolling his kids in taekwondo classes, he decided to enroll himself and his wife, too. Instead of sending the kids to take the class, they all did it together! What started out as just another activity for the kids turned into an unforgettable shared experience that has gone on weekly for a few years already.

Kids don't want their parents to be only their lawgiver, their banker, or their cook. They want to have fun together.

For instance, Joyce loves to cook, so she gets our kids right in there to help from the time they are young. I, on the other hand, love to play basketball, so guess what I do with my teenage boys now whenever we get some free time?

Also, in our home, we have a "movie night" tradition where we all cuddle around popcorn and a flick. The movie typically generates discussion that can last anywhere from a few days or weeks to a few months or years! One of our favorite activities is hiking, but we have also done rock climbing, gone to the trampoline park, and generally have done interesting and challenging things together.

If your sons and daughters are having fun at home, as they grow they won't *only* seek good times outside. You will have planted a seed that will someday sprout in their own families. They will come to define "home" as a haven, a place of peace, a place of laughter, and a place of fun.

I just finished an informal camp with my teenage boys. Being their school holidays, we planned a series of fun events for them and their friends and classmates. We did an educational trek, made tie-dye T-shirts, had a sand castle building contest, set up an "amazing race," and did BBQ and overnight camping as a finale. The camp was the highlight of their holidays, and they will probably never forget it. They grew closer with their friends, and because I did all of the activities with them, we strengthened our bonds as well. And they felt appreciated. It was completely a win-win situation. It was not hard, not expensive, and yet the return on investment can have generational consequences.

CHEERING THEM ON

When I was a kid, everyone in my family loved sports. And playing on a team can be a really good experience for children growing up. There are a lot of valuable life lessons that can be learned on a baseball diamond or a soccer field! I did not appreciate it at the time, but my parents had to drive my brothers and me around to practices and games, but not only did they never complain about it, they were always there at the games, cheering us on. In fact, my mom was always one of the most passionate fans, bellowing out, "You can do it!" or "Come on, Son!" You could literally hear her voice above the crowd!

I've never forgotten the way she cheered us on. A more "proper" woman probably would have felt self-conscious that she was attracting a lot of attention. None of that mattered to Mom. It was all about us. She was going to make sure that we understood she and Dad were there for us. My dad was more meek and subtle, but I would go out into the fray night after night and give 100 percent because I knew that he was watching and wholeheartedly supporting me.

With them around, it was never about winning the game. Sure, we all wanted to win, and we fought hard to. But knowing they were there, hearing their cries of support, or getting a pat on the head at the end of a bad game was enough to make it all worth while, win or lose.

I clearly got my parents' genes! I am probably one of the loudest spectators out there when my kids are on the floor or on the pitch. In reality, one of the most important roles we can play in the lives of our children is for them to know that we are behind them, on or off the field. We may not "hurrah!" when they get good grades or when they perform well. But whatever our children are doing, they need to know that we are there in the crowds, watching over them with pride in our hearts and praise on our lips. We only notice it more during those sporting competitions when the crowds are shouting at the top of their voices. Come on Moms and Dads, lift up your voice. Your son or daughter is worth it!

ENCOURAGEMENT

One of the best gifts we can give to our children does not come wrapped with a bow on it. This gift is not something that is only given on special occasions. It won't cost you a penny. And unlike so many other gifts, it will not be put away in a closet once the novelty is worn off. It cannot be broken, get rusty, or grow mold. It needs no batteries. It's the gift of encouragement.

The word *encouragement* literally means to put courage into, to inspire with courage, and to foster confidence. As parents, simply by virtue of the kind of relationship we have with our children, we have access to the means of building strength into our sons and daughters to face difficulties and challenges. We wield a tool that can make them stand tall when others around them are sitting, an instrument that will stimulate them to overcome fears and opposition. Instead of bowing to peer pressure, we even can enable them to provide leadership to others around them.

Unfortunately, many parents never discover the power of encouragement. We tend to point out our children's faults and remind them of their failures. We do not interact with them upfront or midstream, but rather only at the conclusion of their efforts and projects. When results are less than ideal, our criticism rains down like hail upon their vulnerable spirits.

The wise parent recognizes that words of praise and support along the way are like the people who line the streets during a marathon, cheering for the runners and providing them with water throughout the race. Too many of us only wait at the finish line looking at our watches, unaware of the fact that we were needed to give them "water" along the way. When they don't live up to expectations or give up, our disappointment reads like a neon sign saying, "I'm not surprised. I didn't think you could do it."

I once heard an Olympic sprinter say that he was shocked to discover that, while kneeling at the block for the finals of his race, the thought that entered his mind just before takeoff was, *I wonder whether Dad is watching?*

Your children need *your* encouragement. It emboldens them to face life's challenges, big and small. Let your children know that you are their biggest and best supporter. Your gift will be one that will never break or rust, and it will never, ever be forgotten.

A FATHER'S LETTER

Steven and Natalie are a dynamic father/daughter team from Singapore. Unlike many of her peers, Natalie didn't grow up doubting whether or not her parents were there for her.

Below is a letter Steven wrote to Natalie as an adult, followed by a letter from her back to him, including the words, "I truly believe that I am the woman I am today because of the time and effort that you have spent on me." Wow!

———

My Darling Princess,

I vividly remember the day I laid my eyes on you for the very first time. You were not exactly attractive when we first met; you had mucus and blood all over your body. And yet I remember thinking: *I have never seen a more beautiful girl.* I was there to receive you when you came into this world.

As a first-time father, I did my best to care for, teach, and guide you along life's paths. I made many mistakes because you were my "guinea pig." But then, you were a fine specimen, and I did not have to deviate too much from the many books I read about parenting. Still, I had to gingerly wade through those years of teaching and putting the values that I considered important into your heart.

One parenting book I read in your early years said that girls would grow up confident and possess self-respect if their father constantly showed them love. For that reason, I dated you often to let you know that you were so loved that you need not look for love elsewhere, until it was time for you to find the right man for your life.

I remember the time when I used your graduation from junior college as an excuse to buy you a ring to put on your middle finger. You suspected that I had another motive besides just celebrating your graduation. You were right. I specifically told you that as long as the ring remained on your middle finger, you had to stay chaste, to keep yourself pure for your future husband on your wedding night.

A few years later, when you were seriously dating, I reminded you to be virtuous and you "rebuked" me, saying, "Dad, have some trust in yourself. You have taught me all these values over the years, surely I will keep them." I am proud of you!

During the years of "father bringing up child and child bringing up father," we made many mistakes. You could not understand why I had to ground you or insisted that you be home before a certain time at night. You argued but lost each time you disagreed, and then you cried. Yet you abided by my rules. Finally, after all these years, you understand.

I love you, always and stronger still,
Dad

―――――

THE DAUGHTER'S RESPONSE

―――――

Dear Daddy,

You were the first man I ever knew and loved. While I certainly do not remember meeting you in my blood-filled, mucousy glory, I do remember a loving and patient father who was (and still is) always there for me, no matter what. More importantly you were the first man to love me unconditionally for who I am, in spite of what I do or say.

As a young child, I remember being very playful. I never wanted to wear pants, choosing to run around the house in my T-shirt and underwear. In an attempt to incentivize me (I'm sure you got it from one of those parenting books), you told me that if you came home and saw me wearing pants, you would give me a star. Once I collected multiple stars, I would get a treat of my choice.

I never liked the idea of wearing pants but really loved the idea of having a treat. Hence, I learned to recognize the sound of the gates opening and your car driving into the garage so that I would always have enough time to run upstairs, put on my pants, and greet you with loving arms. I suppose I wasn't very honest then, but I can truthfully tell you that one of the highlights of my day was running into your arms at the end of the day to greet you and give you a huge hug.

Your belief in incentivizing good behavior continued even when I was in primary school. I remember your "treat" cards. If I behaved, I would get the opportunity to choose from a deck of cards with treats written on them. It could be something as trivial as an ice-cream treat to a day at the zoo, and the most awesome of all, any activity of my choice!

While these small but thoughtful gestures were highly appreciated, what I am most thankful for was the fact that you made the effort to spend quality time with me. Thank you for the solo trips including that trip to the zoo (I still remember the picture with the orangutan), a boat ride along Singapore River with my brother (I still have the tickets!), and the daddy and daughter date to Disney on Ice (I still have that photo of us with Donald Duck)!

We had joy and fun in the sun!

I really enjoyed those precious moments and now, having grown up, I appreciate your efforts even more as I now know that it takes a lot of courage and effort for fathers to agree to bring their children out, alone. Not many fathers do that, but you did.

I am truly thankful for your holding closely to the belief that girls will grow up confident and possess self-respect if their father shows them love constantly. I truly believe that I am the woman I am today because of the time and effort that you have spent on me.

More importantly, you taught me the importance of owning up and having the security to admit that I am in the wrong. You were one of the rare parents who were actually comfortable with apologizing to a young twelve-year-old girl when you were in the wrong. Most of my friends' parents refused to admit they were wrong or even apologize; instead, they used the "I am your parent" line.

I believe that it was values like these, and others, which have enabled me to be successful in my career today.

I love you,

Natalie

———

Yes, times have changed. Some of these changes have made life more difficult, complex, and challenging. This has contributed to climbing divorce rates, excessive rebellious behavior, and an increasing number of broken and dysfunctional homes. The fact that forming bonds of friendship with our children is now an acceptable practice is one of the most positive and hopeful changes that has become a part of this generation. I can truly say for Joyce and me, the friendships we have with our older children are among our greatest rewards in life.

If we capitalize on this potential, finding common ground and building bridges to our children's hearts, we will release a force that can reverse many of the other trends and present-day realities that make our job as parents heart-wrenching in these troubled times. Among the pots at the end of your parenting "rainbow" may be a letter from your own son or daughter some day. It may read something like this:

————

Dear Dad (or Mom),

Thank you for taking the time for me, and for taking me out on those DDD/MDDs. Thank you for caring enough to find out what is important to me and for building bridges to my heart. Thank you for all the times you encouraged me and for the ways you supported me. Thank you so much for being my friend.

I love you,
Your Daughter (or Son)

————

PUT IT TO WORK

- **If you have not been taking your sons and daughter out for "dates," and by that I mean one-on-one, please start.** It is simply one of the most meaningful things you can do as a parent. It can have an impact on so many other aspects of your parent/child relationship.

- **Find out what your kids are interested in, and do it together!** Whether it is cooking, or a sport, or a hobby, friends like to do things together.

Discover what you can do with your sons and daughters that you all enjoy—and do it!

- I can still hear my mom's voice above the crowds cheering me on when I was on the field or court during games. **Settle it in your heart today: I will be my child's biggest supporter.** They are going to tell others that I was always a great encouragement to them.

Part Three

HORSE QUALITIES

Horses are powerful and majestic. In order for them to be enjoyed, they have to be tamed and trained to reach their full potentials. Our children have immense capacity to accomplish many things in life. Like the horse, they need to find true strength through knowing discipline and restraint. The horse qualities in this last section are: courage, discipline, responsibility, and forgiveness.

Chapter Ten

PEER PRESSURE

*If you don't want to be average, don't rush into doing
what the crowd is doing.*[42]

— CONSTANCE CHUKS FRIDAY

I remember watching some tremendous thunderstorms when I was young. During one storm, while at a friend's house, I even saw a couple of massive, one-hundred-year-old elm trees come crashing to the ground when the winds were particularly strong. Later, after the storm, we went out to inspect the damage. During this harrowing experience, I will never forget what my friend's dad said as we looked over one of those giant trees. "This one came down," he said, "because its roots were too shallow to support such a big tree."

Teens experience a different kind of a storm. We call it *peer pressure*. Sometimes, the pressure can seem so great, like gale-force winds hitting those majestic trees that have no natural means of defense. Though some swaying and rustling are unavoidable, the critical matter for teenagers is: Do they have a deep enough root system to keep them from succumbing to the cyclones of opinions, trends, and taunts coming at them from all sides?

ROOT SYSTEMS

Peer pressure *is the influence you feel from a person or group of people to do something you might not otherwise consider doing.* It is our job as parents to make sure that our children's "root systems" are strong enough to withstand intense pressure. Kids "bend" to the winds of peers when they do not feel accepted, understood, or listened to at home.

When we as parents fail to affirm our children, and praise them for their achievements, they begin to look to their classmates to provide them with a sense of self-worth that should have come from us. When we don't do the kinds of things with our sons and daughters that give them a clear sense of who they are and where they are going, with assurances we will be by their sides to help them to get there, they start to look to their peers who are here today and gone tomorrow. The results can be disastrous. Kids may be coerced into experimenting with drugs, sex, or deviant behavior.

Joyce loves plants. She loves to get her hands in the soil. When her plants do well, there is a sweet contentment that settles upon her. If the plant is outgrowing the pot, and the roots become too cramped, my wife will not hesitate to take them out, retaining much of the original soil, and then transplant the plant into a larger pot wherein its roots have plenty of room to "breathe." She will add some new soil, and sometimes put in some special plant nutrients to nudge it along.

Our children are also like these plants, and we are their gardeners. We have to keep a watchful eye on them, observing whether the leaves are turning yellow or the plant has become droopy, blighted, or moldy. The wise gardener doesn't try to *make* the plant grow. He doesn't introduce dramatic changes, but he gradually "mothers" it by slight changes to the amount of water or sunlight. He inspects the other plants in the surroundings to make sure there are not any diseases that could affect the healthy ones. He understands that the real story of the plant is what lies beneath the surface. You can employ many different kinds of interventions, but at the end of the day, a plant will only ever be as healthy and strong as its roots.

So the parental challenge is to create the right environmental factors to make our "plants" (children) grow in a balanced and wholesome way. We can't "make" them grow any more than the gardener can "make" his favorite veggies grow. We must know when to add some sunlight or gently pull them back into a shaded area. Sunlight is akin to the warmth and emotional security we surround them with in the home. The shaded areas are the harmful things from which we shelter them.

Roots speak of origins, of foundations, or of substance. We need to instill in our sons and daughters a strong sense of *who they are, where they come from,* and *where they are going.* Do they feel connected to extended family? Are you having discussions with them about your values, your beliefs? Can they articulate these for themselves? Do you have a family vision, and do they know where they fit into it? The more effective we are at building these in, the deeper their roots will be. Our children will be more self-confident and self-aware. When the winds come, they won't topple over. Rather than being influenced by others, they can influence those around them—for good!

A TEEN SHARES HER STRUGGLES

Shania is fifteen and from the high-pressured nation of Singapore. She is grateful that her parents have invested in the kinds of things that have built a firm foundation in her life, empowering her to resist the temptation to conform to social whims:

———

My parents have always been encouraging and generous, knowing when to comfort or reward me and my sisters. Similarly, they knew when to draw the line, be it with regards to our demands or behavior. One common phrase used among us sisters when we tried to convince our parents into granting our requests was, "But my friends can, so why can't I?"

Already at a young age, people feel a need to prove their worth by fitting in with their environment. It seems as though not conforming to the standards of the norm makes us feel inferior. We want to be accepted, but at what cost?

Being young and innocent, children are susceptible to picking up bad habits or traits from whatever they are exposed to. One of the easy targets is using foul language. My parents were strict with what we were allowed to watch, sing and say, even if we reasoned that our friends could do or say these things. In primary school, I remember so many of my friends using expletives; some were vulgarities—which I knew were downright wrong to say. Thinking it was "cool," I felt pressured to swear in order to be accepted by my friends.

In the car one day, my sister and I were playing a hand game, and when I lost one of those "bleeps" slipped out. My dad immediately asked what I had said. I knew I was in deep trouble. This time, I didn't retort, probably because I already knew that I had really blown it. I waited to see how my parents would respond. What made me respect my parents' stand was their explanation as to why they did not approve of using that word. They did not scold me, but showed me that it was not something glorifying or uplifting to say. It is honorable to resist saying or doing anything impure or unedifying. This had such an impression on me that, since that first time I used bad language, I was never tempted to ever say anything like that again.

Another area where I have felt a lot of pressure is in trying to make myself more attractive. Because my peers were constantly doing things to improve their looks, I just couldn't resist the temptation to compare myself with them. I struggled with feeling inadequate. And although I was greatly disappointed at times, I also didn't find it easy to confide in my parents about it. And yet somehow they seemed to know.

Whenever I would feel especially down about it, my

parents would remind me of how proud they were of me! Their constant words of affirmation kept me strong and prevented me from taking unnecessary actions to try to improve my appearance, which I surely would have regretted doing afterwards. Frankly, because of my parents' encouragement, I just haven't felt the need to have to prove my worth; neither have I questioned my true identity.

It may seem unfair that they were so strict, but I am glad they brought us up with limits. Peer pressure surely gets to everyone, but because my parents were firm in their values and did not let us compromise our standards, we have learned to guard ourselves against temptation and understand that our self-worth is not measured by the things we are enticed to do to please others, but rather, by how many enticements we can boldly resist.

––––––––

OPEN 24/7

Children need to know that they always have access to their parents. There should never be a time when a child feels as though the door to his mom and dad is closed. On the contrary, when my son or my daughter knocks on our door, he or she should know that the sign reads, "Open 24/7."

Unfortunately, many children knock on the door that has another sign hanging there. "Busy." "Come back later." "Take a number." "On vacation." What we as parents need to understand is that children don't need to have a "reason" to come in. Their problem or question doesn't have to be earth-shattering. It doesn't have to be a crisis. In fact, it doesn't have to be anything. Maybe all he or she needs is a hug, a smile, or a pat on the head. Maybe the question is not the reason for coming at all, but a smokescreen of what's really happening inside: a longing for affection or affirmation. I find even my older kids will at times just come and sit on my lap—for nothing!

Of course, there are also real problems or questions that are itching for an answer, too. They start out simple and become more complex as our children grow. But each step along the way, our kids need to know they can come to us— anywhere, anytime. Otherwise, if children find that our door is closed, they will begin to knock elsewhere. Little girls may knock on the door of the first boy who shows an interest in them, and then the next, and the next. Little boys may knock on the door of the boy in the gang who is a little older and cooler than they are. Before you know it, your daughter has formed a certain approach to life, and your son has become trapped in a web from which escape is costly.

Being a parent does not mean you have to know everything. But it does mean that you have to be available. It means your children know that your door is always open 24/7.

HELP YOUR KIDS CHOOSE GOOD FRIENDS

We must be aware of the people who have an influence over and are placing peer pressure upon our children. On whose doors *are* your children knocking? With whom do they associate? Who are their buddies? Who are the people outside of the home who are having the greatest impact on the way they think or the values they embrace? Who are their "heroes"? What about their Internet "friends"?

Three thousand years ago, King David of Israel penned these oft-quoted and timeless words: "Blessed is the man who walks not in the counsel of the ungodly, nor stands in the way of sinners, nor sits in the seat of the scornful."[43] Simply stated, King David was saying that the people with whom we associate really make a difference in the quality of our lives.

We cannot just assume our children will choose friends wisely. In fact, wrong choices can be disastrous. What if the new "friend" who is a few years older is really a drug dealer? What if an older boy, or someone engaged in an Internet chatroom, is just targeting your unsuspecting daughter for illicit sex? While these are extreme cases, they are also all too common in our day and highlight the need for us as parents to be vigilant.

It is important to guide our sons and daughters in making friendship decisions. Joyce and I have made it a practice not to casually allow our children to spend time at other children's homes until we know more about them. So we will often invite these children to our home first, and in the process observe them as well as engage them in conversation. We take the opportunity to get to know the parents as well. One of the questions we ask our children's teachers has to do with the kids with whom they are hanging out at school. This is not something to be casual and passive about.

Pay special attention to times when your children are naturally at risk. Is your son or daughter going through puberty? Are you moving to a new area? Are they transitioning from one school to another? Has a close friend or family member recently died or a classmate committed suicide? Have you had some heart-to-heart talks with them as they prepare to go off to college? They will more easily succumb to pressure when they are emotionally and psychologically weak.

We all need to talk with our children about the importance of seeking out quality friendships. What things should you be looking for?

Here are some ideas:

- Are their friends honest and respectful of adults?

- Do they "bend the rules" and encourage others to do so also?

- Are they lazy?

- Do they pick on or bully other kids?

- Do they curse, or are they constantly critical of others?

- Do they talk about home-life disparagingly, or does home seem to be an unhappy place for them?

Teach your children that to search for good friends who encourage them to become all that they can be is a lifelong pursuit. I was recently speaking with the co-founder of a very successful business chain. He told me of a life-changing decision he had made a few years back. He decided to make some new friends! He described sitting in a coffee shop with his old buddies and suddenly realizing that they still talked about the same things whenever they had gotten together for the past twenty years! He perceived that his "friends" were in no way challenging him to become a better person, or strive to reach his personal goals. When he set his mind to pursue a few quality friends, he was rewarded beyond his expectation.

As adults we can look back over a lifetime and see how our friendships have impacted us, positively or negatively. Find the time to share your valuable lessons with your sons and daughters.

We have made it a priority to teach our children about the importance of choosing good friends. We hope they won't live to regret their choices, either because they became involved in things which were painful, illicit, or unsavory, or because they awake one day and discover that twenty years could have been better spent. Either way, as parents we need to be sober; the friends our children make can be game-changers.

With whom our children "sit," "walk," and "stand" is important! All of us are deeply impacted by the people with whom we associate. As true as this is for adults, it is even more critical for our children who are impressionable and vulnerable to the pressures exerted upon them by their peers. Find out more about your son's and daughter's friends. Don't delay; start today.

"I DARE YOU!"

The following quotation is true figuratively:

> There are two kinds of people in this world: those who follow the popular majority, and those who possess good sense. In other words, you can either let the crowd steer you right over a cliff, or you can stop to peer beyond the brink and see how a fall will likely end in tragedy.[44]

It can also be true literally. If exuberance is one of the strengths of youth, then a lack of evaluating consequences is a weakness. I am sure we all have some things we regret from our youth. Some things we did may even seem downright foolish from our adult perch. It is our duty as parents to warn our children when situations may turn dangerous. Why subject them to painful memories or even something worse?

Did you ever notice that young ones are constantly chiding each other—"I dare you"? It may be something as innocent as a dare to kiss the cute girl who sits in the third row; or it could be to steal a magazine from the store, or jump a precarious distance to proddings of "It's easy—what are you, chicken?"! Are our children prepared to do what's right in these situations? Have we taught them to weigh consequences?

While writing this chapter, news broke of five teens from Michigan in the U.S. who are facing the prospects of spending the rest of their lives in prison.[45] For what, you ask? Ages 15 through 17, these boys were dropping rocks off a bridge overpass onto the highway traffic below. What began as a dare, ended in the murder of a 32-year-old man who left behind a loving wife and five-year-old son.

Then there were the three guys from my high school, all one year ahead of me, who tried to race their car across the train tracks *before* the train passed. They had sped up, but not fast enough. The collision killed all three of them instantly. I wonder if the conversation before impact had been, "Come on, Joe, I dare you!"?

Maybe you know someone who died on a dare? Or maybe he lived, but one wrong choice in the face of pressure from peers resulted in scars that he will carry over a lifetime.

When I was young, I nearly became a statistic. I had built up a reputation as a high diver: thirty, forty, fifty feet jumps. Sometimes, it was not the height but the difficulty. I took one dare too many, and hit bottom—head first! At first I thought I had gotten off unscathed, but as headaches increased and I had to drop out of sports, the doctors found I had a slight fracture in a vertebra in my neck. I could have been paralyzed for life! I recovered, but I never forgot it. I turned it into a message to share with my kids. "Foolish choices can come back to haunt you. Don't live your life on a dare!"

BOUNDARIES

We live on the nineteenth floor, with a magnificent balcony from which we have a view of the city. As much as I love it, I would not stay here even one day if the balcony did not have a railing. I did not buy this house because of the railings, but I would not live here one day without them.

My kids need railings, too, but not just the type that keep them safe on our balcony. They need railings that say, "This is not the kind of friend with whom you should be spending time," or "This is the hour the lights in your room need to be out," or "This is not the kind of movie you should be watching." We would never live in a house without a railing, and yet we often overlook the dangers that exist for children in a home where no boundaries are identified for behavior, attitudes, habits, or relationships. When people fall off these "balconies," they might not break bones, but they may be "crippled" in other ways.

Such is the case for a dear friend of mine whose daughter had a one-night fling with her "boyfriend" and got pregnant. If we don't realize that our children are under tremendous duress to conform to pressure from friends to become sexually active as teenagers, we are quite out of touch. If we naïvely think they aren't tempted, we have our heads in the sand.

Teen boys often see having sex as a receiving a kind of trophy. Girls, too, are not immune to the hook-up culture that lures them in. *Movies and social media are conditioning them to believe that this is normal,* and to be inactive is prudish, nerdy, and embarrassing.

Fortunately, because of their family convictions, my friend's daughter remained single and refused to abort the baby. This disastrous choice could have left an emotional and psychological scar on her for life. True, the baby is beautiful, intelligent, and happy. And yet everything dramatically changed for the whole family that day.

Jobs changed. They sold or gave away most of their possessions and relocated far away to start a new life. They had to start from scratch to meet new friends. Since the baby came, someone has had to stay at home to take care of her. Nearly all their future plans were put on hold or cancelled entirely. The shockwaves from this one unbridled decision had left many casualties.

How does your "balcony" look? Is it secure? Have you checked to make sure the railings are not broken or bars removed? If we consider security to be of utmost importance to our children, then we must not forget to erect firm boundaries for them to live in. This is not something to leave to chance. The risks are too high.

POSITIVE PRESSURE

We live in a materialistic age where people measure success by how much money you earn, what kind of car you drive, or which neighborhood you live in. We are constantly being bombarded by a media that feeds on this warped value system. Although we should know better, the influence of this buy-your-way-to-happiness culture affects all of us and is a subtle threat to a healthy family life.

In reality, things break, get rusty and out of date, or their novelty wears off. To try to substitute the most valued things of life—such as quality time, a meaningful heart-to-heart talk, or even just a fun time together with a toy or a gift or a gadget—is an insult to our humanity.

My son doesn't need to have the newest, flashiest sneakers to wear for his basketball game. He needs me to be there in the audience cheering him on. My daughter doesn't need to be motivated to study hard because I will give her fifty dollars for a good mark. She needs me to sit with her and help her wrestle with her difficult homework assignment.

Just because we live in a materialistic age does not mean we have to fall into its trap. My children need me, not just the things that I give them. The best way to combat negative pressure that comes from peers is, well, to apply positive pressure that comes from us parents.

Positive pressure can also come from the quality friends whom we have guided them to find. Or maybe we are a part of a faith-based community or pursue a hobby with others who have strong family values. This "pressure" does not press down on our children, compelling them to conform to expectations and external demands. It comes from underneath, giving them a push, or a lift. And it comes from inside, from the roots, from a heart that has been made confident and bold. When the crowd is going one way, they will not blindly follow, but with determination and conviction they will stand their ground, or even forge a new path in which others may end up following them.

Gravity is a kind of pressure that can either be our worst enemy or our bosom friend. If you fall off a roof, you surely will not consider gravity a welcome companion on the way down. But if you are in an airplane, the pressure downward is what is captured to propel you to fly.

Peers often demand unanimity and conformity. The tension usually exerts itself on teenagers to be "in" and not "out," to do what's popular or to be cool.

But the pages of history are not lined with conformists and crowd-pleasers. The ones we honor and enshrine are like Martin Luther, who changed the course of history because he could not stay silent in the face of corrupt and misguided religious practices, or his namesake Martin Luther King, whose courage helped to revolutionize laws and cultural attitudes about human rights.

Like gravity, peer pressure can also galvanize our children's resolves to rise above what is average. The pressure to do well on exams can make one child anxious and underperform, while at the same time motivate another to excellence. Whether its effect is positive or negative is largely determined by how well we have prepared our children to handle and harness pressure. It starts at home.

THE EIFFEL TOWER

The Eiffel Tower is one of the most recognizable landmarks on the planet. Built as a grand entrance to the 1889 World's Fair, the tower receives hundreds of thousands of visitors every year and is a favorite spot for lovers to rendezvous. It wasn't always beloved. It was built in the face of fierce opposition.

A group of leading artists and writers, including the author of *The Three Musketeers,* Alexander Dumas, filed a petition that read: "We writers, painters, sculptors, architects, and lovers of the beauty of Paris, do protest with all our vigor and all our indignation, in the name of French taste and endangered French art and history, against the useless and monstrous Eiffel Tower."[46]

History vindicated Alexander Eiffel. In 1889, he was roundly condemned. Today, he is universally praised. His story shows us that what matters is not the opinions others have of us and what we do. These will change according to what is culturally fashionable. What matters is holding on to our values and what we believe. When we impart this tenacity and resilience to our children, they will not sway or wobble when the winds of their peers blow on them any more than the Eiffel Tower will rock on Paris's most breezy nights.

Like the mighty Eiffel, the towering elms and majestic oaks that still line those same streets of my hometown have not bowed to winds, or storms, or blizzards. Their roots are healthy and unperturbed by the gusts of public and peer opinions after all these years. If you plant your sons and daughters in the soil of affirmation and self-awareness, they too will not sway or crack in the face of prevailing public or peer opinions. Let's not raise our children to be average. We owe them more than that.

PUT IT TO WORK

- **Do your kids feel connected to their "roots" (extended family, ancestors)?** Are you having discussions with them about your values, your beliefs? Can they articulate these for themselves? Do you have a family vision, and do they know where they fit into it?

- **Sit down and have an honest conversation with your sons and daughters** about the things for which they feel especially pressured by their peers right now. It might be helpful to talk about your own struggles with these things when you were young, apply your own experiences to build a bridge to them, and show them that there are real rewards to resisting.

- **Find a good time to talk with your children about their friendships.** Apart from being more observant, take steps to make helping your kids choose good friends a priority. Go back to the "Help Your Kids Choose Good Friends" section and review the ideas I have mentioned of things for which you will want to be on the lookout.

- **Make sure your children are confident enough to stand up to a dare.**

- **Talk to your children about having the right kinds of "pressure,"** which I call "positive pressure," in their lives. If they don't have positive pressure at work in their lives, commit to creating it. You will be glad you did!

Chapter Eleven

REBELLION IS A BUMMER

Rebellion. When people ask why life is so difficult, the answer can be summed up in that one word.[47]

— RICK WARREN

The Fast and the Furious Franchise is Universal Picture's largest grossing movie series ever, amassing a mind-boggling four billion U.S. dollars. Translated into no less than twenty-four of the world's top languages, these movies have literally and figuratively raced to the top of Hollywood's action film mountain, filling the globe not just with startlingly vivid hi-tech entertainment and adrenaline rushes; they have a message, too:

> Live life in the fast lane! You only live once, so take it to the edge, even if you have to break the law to do it. And it doesn't matter when some people become the collateral damage of your "mission." In fact, it's okay, because the

end justifies the means. Never mind that you commit a few crimes along the way, at least you have a high moral standard about your friends—you will be loyal to the death. Rebellion is fun! The world is out there for you to enjoy. What matters is not how you do it, but that you do it with passion—with fury!

If someone wanted to come to our schools and give a talk entitled, "Rebellion Is Really Cool!" he would never get a foot in the door. Unwittingly, we may have kept him from our schools yet invited him into our living rooms! Packaged ingeniously as "entertainment," muscle-bound and bikini-clad celebrities have become the gurus and prophets of our generation. Subtly, the lines that defined the boundaries of right and wrong, or good and bad, have blurred into oblivion. Rather than passing down a moral compass with a true north (N) to guide them along life's journey, N is now whatever has a "#" in front of it, and that changes from week to week.

I have talked with many parents who now *expect* their children to rebel, as though it has become an acceptable and natural part of growing up! I have also talked with others who were genuinely shocked when one of my kids *didn't* rebel. They talk as though the word *teenage* does not describe an age grouping but a fearful and unavoidable, behavioral chicken pox that lasts for years and for which there is no immunization. But is it really the case that we must capitulate and resign ourselves to years of heartache, hoping only to manage the fallout of pain and destruction? Do we bury our heads in the sand when our kids reach thirteen, hoping they pop out ten years later, having survived frat initiations and spring breaks unscathed enough to get a job and become "normal" again?

A "NORMAL" TEENAGE STORY

Most of our children survived the teen years without many of the bumps and bruises of their peers. Tabitha fell briefly into the swamp of rebellion and fortunately was able to pull out of her funk and get back on the right track. The sting of that time has been a warning to her along the way. She has also warned others not to fall into this swamp. She is now in her last year of pre-law at university and doing brilliantly!

————

As a teenager, I juggled the task of figuring out who I was and how I fit into the world. We had moved around a lot, and I had never really attended public schools in the U.S. until eighth and ninth grade. The first thing I did was make "friends." The problem was that, at that age, you really don't think about the influence others have on you. I went through a period where I wanted to do my own thing. It seemed like a teenage "rite of passage" to be rebellious for a while, to experience life! As the saying goes, "yolo—you only live once."

I gravitated towards the wrong crowd, went to parties, and got involved in shallow relationships with boys. I thought all of this would help me feel happy and good about myself. But in fact, I felt a greater dissatisfaction because I had to compartmentalize my life and would alter how I would act and talk around different groups of friends. I wasn't being real. Worst of all was the fact I had to go behind my parents back and betray their trust in order to do these things. I knew I wasn't honoring them, and the peace I once knew was slipping through my fingers.

Eventually, I got caught in my sin, and my parents sat me down and talked to me about it. They took me out of school, took away my phone and social media accounts, and basically put me on total lockdown. At this point, I really had two options: 1) I could harbor bitterness towards my parents and say, "They just don't understand what I'm going through," or 2) I could apologize and realize that what I was doing was wrong. I wisely chose the latter!

————

THE TEEN SCENE

Young people today are constantly bombarded with tacit and blatant invitations to cross over the line into rebellion. In our wireless world, Hollywood and Madison Avenue don't even need to run a cable to connect to your children's bedrooms. Images are flashing into their consciousness in musical tones from every direction at all hours of the day. Unsuspecting kids will have been Swiftified long before they realize it. When they are fed Miley Cyrus before cereal in the morning, we shouldn't fool ourselves into thinking they are only listening to music. There's a lifestyle being preached in these lyrics. Twerking is not just a dance move; it's a symbol of war against traditional values.

What was once fringe is now mainstream; things that were taboo are now touted. The average youth not only cannot swim against the current, but they don't even know why they should. The gestation of the media's constant buzz will give birth to attitudes created in its likeness right around the time kids hit middle school. Resisting its power may range from seeming futile to outright foolish.

Korean Hip Hop artist PSY's "Gangman Style" has had more than three billion views on YouTube. This is by far the most hits of any YouTube video ever. We are fooling ourselves if we think that this overload of information is not having a telltale effect of the cultures and attitudes of our youth.

I am not suggesting this is an entirely new phenomenon. Teenagers have been pushing the boundaries wider and wider for a long time. I still remember the days of Woodstock and the emergence of a counterculture generation in America in 1969. Before that, there were Elvis and James Dean, the iconic "Rebel Without A Cause" of the 1950s. The point here is not that we are witnessing something totally new in terms of a trend for this age group; it is that there is a qualitative difference between the size and scope, in the depth and expansiveness of its influence during our time. To use the same yardstick to measure those times and these is like trying to download modern apps on the first generation of Atari computers! You will experience system failure. The rules have changed.

Neither am I casting blame. This generation of teens did not create the forces that have been unleashed against them. Neither am I suggesting they are all negative. (I routinely ask my ten-year-old to help me figure out how to use my gadgets!) But what is absolutely critical is that we understand each other, for only by means of understanding will we breed appreciation.

Twenty-five hundred years ago, a Chinese sage wisely said:

$$知彼知己，百战不殆$$

Roughly translated, this means, if you know others (i.e., one's "enemies"), and you know yourself, you will remain unscathed though you fight a hundred battles. By this I am not calling the younger generation the enemy! I'm simply saying that we must obtain an accurate assessment of what we are up against in order to be prepared to face and overcome the difficulties and challenges arrayed before us.

MY REBEL DAYS

I had my rebellious days, too. I know what it is like to "live on the edge." We thought our parties were just a part of the normal "fun and games" of growing up, so we partied hard. If there was another way to feel like one could fit in, it was obscured by the fog of youthful zeal. It appeared that those who were making it to the top of the popularity pile were the ones who embraced a bit of the dark side, who dared let the beasts in their hearts out of their cages. It wasn't just the beverages that were intoxicating; it was the opportunity to live with "independence" and abandon. I wish someone had warned me beforehand that it was false advertising.

I'll never forget the time I was riding in the front seat of a massively overcrowded car when my wild-eyed, drunken classmate hit 120 miles per hour driving on winding dirt roads. Neither stopping nor slowing down at intersections was a part of the plan. How we survived I'll never know. At some point, and maybe just in time, I sobered up (literally *and* figuratively). But I almost did not live to write about it.

One day, while in a drunken state, I foolishly dove into a mountain swimming hole and hit my head on the bottom, blacking out for an instant upon impact. When I began to experience regular headaches weeks later, numerous visits to the doctors revealed I had suffered a hairline fracture in my neck. This easily could have left me paralyzed or dead. And as for our joyride, I wish I could say it was all fun and games, but the "laughter" turned to deep searchings of heart when three of our schoolmates died in a car crash in similar circumstances a year later.

Rebellion wasn't turning out to be so much fun after all. By the time I graduated from high school, I was heading in a completely different direction, having left behind my reckless, shortsighted ways.

CONSEQUENCES

When parents enter into the teenage world, they have to learn a whole new vocabulary. But there is one word which is difficult to find in a teenager's dictionary—*consequences*.

"Consequences? What are those, right? Sounds rather antiquated, belonging back there with thees and thous," they may say. "If you look hard enough, you can find it in the teen thesaurus under 'antonym for awesome, cool, and rad.' It has a synonym too, right? Oh yes, *boring!*"

I realize this whole idea might burst a few bubbles, but

actions *do* have consequences. People *do* dive into shallow pools and end up in wheelchairs for the rest of their lives. Cars *do* skid out of control and wind up upside down in fields. Pranks *do* go wrong. Kids *do* get caught breaking the law and end up in prison. People *do* get addicted to drugs.

And girls *do* get pregnant. Okay, they don't in the movies, but Main Street is not Hollywood Boulevard either. Our heroes and idols don't have "accidents," and their obsession with sex certainly looks liberating on MTV. In the virtual world, it's all about guilt-free, mountaintop gratification. In the real world, accidents *do* happen, shame and brokenness *do* abound, and teenage girls *do* get pregnant at alarming rates.

According to the UN Population Fund, "about 16 million girls aged between 15 and 19 years old give birth each year."[48] In the U.S., more than a third of pregnant teens will choose to have an abortion, which equates to 350,000 per year.[49] A million pregnant teenagers a year is not just a blip on the screen of the American statistics bureaus. Whether they choose to keep the baby, or abort, either way, there are real consequences that must be faced.

Basically, there are two choices. Unless they are from one of the 75 nations where abortion is completely (54) or partially (21) illegal, they can choose to have an abortion.[50] Or they can choose to keep their baby, in which case they may raise him or her, or they can give their child up for adoption. It is important for us to understand that neither choice, abortion or keeping the baby, is an easy one, and that both carry a heavy weight of implications.

In the chapter on peer pressure, I mentioned a tragic story

of a friend's daughter who got pregnant. My friend had been posted overseas when his teenage daughter Rachel got pregnant by another expatriate's son (Mark). At the time, both of them had already made plans to pursue further studies back in their homelands. The idea of getting married was tossed around but never really given serious thought. Due to religious convictions, Rachel's parents would not consider abortion, and it was decided that Rachel would have the baby even if it meant she would have to raise the child as a single parent.

In supporting her decision, the parents decided they would return to their homeland with her and help her with the baby in order that she might be able to continue her pursuit of a college degree. Dad quit his job. They sold most of their possessions, packed up the younger siblings, and found an apartment near the university where Rachel planned to study. The other children enrolled in local schools as complete strangers. For a while, Dad found it nearly impossible to find a job.

In time, the baby was born, but not before virtually everything had changed and great personal sacrifices had been made by every member of the family. Of course, the sacrificing didn't end at birth. All lives involved were impacted by the careless actions of two teenagers.

Not everyone is as fortunate as Rachel was to have such supportive parents. Only 2 percent of teen mothers go on to complete a college degree by age thirty. Theirs is a testimony that these kinds of tragedies are survivable, but also a reminder that all those stars who are making their millions selling their fanciful ideals do not represent the real world. They get rich flaunting their provocative videos laced with luscious lyrics, and yet we are the ones who pay, and by that I don't mean just for downloads.

THE ABORTION "DEBATE"

There is another option available in many parts of the world. It's abortion. While the availability of abortion in many parts of the world has dramatically lowered the "risks" or "fallout" from an unwanted pregnancy, the facts betray this propaganda. Whereas the echoes of "It's safe, and easy," and "No one will ever know," ring out from abortion providers (many of whom benefit financially for this "service"), and from boyfriends or others who may stand to suffer embarrassment or upheaval if the pregnancy is not terminated, there are two other strong voices in this matter that are seldom heard.

First, the babies are not given the opportunity to speak. They may well be the greatest victims of all. But even if you consider babies in the womb to be fetuses and not subject to "rights," meaning they do not have a voice in the debate, what about the voices of all of the mothers? Are we really listening to them? If we are, we will certainly hear weeping voices like Elaine's:

> The doctor told me that my nine-week-old baby was nothing more than a sprouted wheat seed. I wanted to believe that lie and be able to forget the pregnancy and get on with my life. What followed the abortion choice were ten years full of addictive behavior, depression, suicidal thoughts, and an inability to bond in relationships.[51]

The number of women who undergo an abortion and suffer psychological and relational turmoil for years and years following the procedure is shocking. Melinda writes, "I took my abortion and stuffed it way down inside. Then I covered it with food, alcohol, drugs and business for the next 32 years, never allowing myself to 'go there' in my mind." Jessica's response is also typical: "To this very day, anxiety, depression, and anger still haunt me." Many relive those tragic moments in recurring nightmares.[52] Others harbor intense resentment and duel daily with guilt and shame.

It's unavoidable. Young people who take risks, whether on highways or in bedrooms, or a myriad of other ways, are playing with fire. They are playing not only with, but against, the odds. And when their "luck" runs short, the resulting pain, regret, and loss can be a thousand times more injurious than the fleeting pleasures they had been seeking.

REBELLION AFFECTS OTHERS

Okay, let's say your kid is a survivor. She doesn't get pregnant, or he doesn't suffer a major accident. One of the great costs of rebellion is the tensions, breakdowns of communication, and strife that are created in a home. Home should be a haven of peace, a shelter from the storms of life, a bedrock of stability under our feet. As good as this ideal sounds, it is not automatic. It takes hard work; in fact, it is only possible as each person in the household does his or her part. This is not the place to point the finger, keep record of wrongs, or retreat to one's corner. Family relationships are a laboratory where we learn to live in harmony with others, to deal with conflict and differences in a constructive way, and to value the perspectives of those closest to you.

One person's rebellion can affect the dynamics of an entire household. Friends will come and go, but we will always have our families. A wise son or daughter recognizes that violating the trust of parents affects much more than having to say "no" to a "friend" who most likely won't be there at the end of this chapter of his or her life. His or her maturity is measured less by doing an adult-like thing (e.g., drinking alcohol or having sex), than it is by acting in an adult-like manner, less by living for the moment than considering how our actions affect our tomorrows. Young people realize their parents and siblings are those who know them best (and still love them!) and who are indispensable companions along life's journey.

WHY REBEL?

So what is it that drives teenagers to take the plunge into defiance? I am reminded of the harrowing scene from *National Geographic* of the wildebeest migration crossing the Mara River of the Serengeti (Kenya, East Africa). Labeled one of the *Seven New Wonders of the World,* more than two million wildebeest, zebras, and gazelles travel hundreds of miles in search of well-watered and green pastures, climaxing in the river crossing where crocodiles lie in wait to prey upon these unsuspecting creatures.

Everything in you wants to warn these animals of the lurking dangers, but like so many teenagers in the world today, they herd into the waters mixed with the blood of their own. The teenage years are best described by the word *definition*. This delicate time, when they are no longer children and have not obtained the maturity of adulthood, calls for deep searchings of soul, where they ask themselves: *Who am I? What will I become? What is my purpose? How can I be accepted?*

In past centuries, definitions were provided by one's family (clan), community, and shared beliefs (religion). As the influence of these institutions and structures has diminished in modern times, and especially in urban settings, definitions are no longer passed down but "discovered." The sway of parents, once dominant, has shifted largely to one's peers; the setting of standards has veered away from the home to the school, and now to the Internet or the streets. The rules are determined by Facebook and Twitter, rather than on tablets of stone or around the kitchen table.

The propensity to find one's niche in the adult world now involves much more experimentation and risk. The choices, once narrow, now appear almost limitless; but this vastness is at least as intimidating as it is exhilarating. It is difficult to get lost in one's backyard; but what about in expansive grasslands? Could it be that the herd instinct, like that which drives the wildebeest, is even stronger in such an urban jungle?

At the very least, we cannot be ignorant of the pressures our teenagers are facing as they pass through the dangerous waters of youth. Not to conform is to face certain scorn, alienation, or worse. Much has been made of bullying in recent years, and for good reason. When bullying is present, out of survival, some children go to great lengths to gain acceptance. Others never recover from the psychological damage it causes, with rising suicide rates and mass shootings a product of the intense struggle kids face in a world that has an increasingly hostile, if not violent, bent.

A rebelling student who would sneak a smoke of a cigarette in times past now has much more ominous things to smoke, or snort, or jab, at his or her fingertips. While peer pressure is nothing new, it is now intensified. As the central role of family and community is displaced by random standards and postmodern blur, definitions become increasingly hard to form and are subjectivized. Philosopher Friedrich Nietzsche astutely anticipated this resulting identity crisis in "The Parable of the Madman," from which the famed expression "God is dead" was coined:

Who gave us the sponge to wipe away the entire horizon? What were we doing when we unchained this earth from its sun? Whither is it moving now? Whither are we moving? Away from all suns? Are we not plunging continually? Backward, sideward, forward, in all directions? Is there still any up or down?[53]

"The Madman" warns us that becoming unchained

seems liberating at first, until all moorings are lost. The fruits of rebellion are the same. "Freedom" to smoke turns to an addiction from which there is no freedom. Sexual "liberation" may express itself in lyrics of, "love, love, love," in songs, and yet in the end have nothing to do with real love, and digress into a very poor substitute. It may even lead people to the false conclusion that love itself is a fantasy, giving rise to disillusionment and dysfunction in relationships over a lifetime.

WHAT'S A PARENT TO DO?

How do parents keep their teenagers from becoming victims of rebellion during those volatile teenage years? A critical thing to bear in mind is that *the seeds of rebellion are sown while they are growing through the formative years leading up to their teens.* When children realize that there are consequences for wrong behavior at every stage of growth, for instance, they will be more likely to consider repercussions of their actions when they become teenagers. While there is no cure-all formula, here are several suggestions:

- **Always communicate unconditional acceptance of your children.** Affirm them often, so that when conflicts arise as they mature, they will still move towards you and not away from you.

- **Be consistent and wise in disciplining your children.** Follow through. When you say there will be a punishment, keep your word. Children who experience boundaries as real also come to understand there is wisdom in and benefits to them.

- **Gradually grant them the independence they desire at the age appropriate time.** This is a skill. To hold the reins too tightly for too long can embitter a child. To hold the reins too loosely and to release them too early can set them up for failure and breed insecurity and mistrust.

- **Communicate, communicate, communicate.** At every stage communication is key. As children mature, communication is paramount. The child who feels like his or her parents hear and understand him or her will not wander far down the road of rebellion. Learn to listen.

- **Have and communicate a plan, and do it.** Achieving the goals of the plan are never automatic. Acceptance is unconditional. Rewards are not. They are a result of well thought out plans and our children's compliance to their part in the process.

- **Continue to do things together.** Find things that are of interest to your children but which can be enjoyed together. I may do sports with my boys, but I also have regular "DDDs" with my girls (Daddy Daughter Dates).

- **Help them with the definitions.** Since teenagers are seeking definitions, guide them in discovering them. Be careful not to *tell* them the answers you want to hear. The skillful parent knows that, when they discover the answer, this ownership is not easily taken from them. Do not push them to accept your definitions. They will likely push back.

CONCLUSION

Rebellion is not all that it is dressed up to be by the media and friends! It is a very costly form of "freedom," for in order to purchase rebellion you mortgage yourself out to strife and tension and separation. What it offers, it cannot give, like the carrot on a stick. Worse, it can even be like a recurring nightmare, or like a hard-drive that is virus-stricken without a cure.

The thrill and allurement of Ferraris barreling around hairpin curves, whizzing past scores of frenzied onlookers, streaking towards a makeshift finish line at frightening speeds are a part of the fantasy and imagination of young minds everywhere. Hundreds of millions have been mesmerized by *The Fast and the Furious* on film, but how many have downloaded the magical feeling captured on the silver screen once their feet have touched the gas pedal in revved up reliving of the adrenalin rush stirred up by these movies? How many, too, will not live to tell of how much "fun" they had when their cars wound up upside down in a field somewhere?

Sadly, living life in the fast lane is not all that it is drummed up to be. As fun as it is advertised to be, rebellion can be costly—very costly. Meadow Walker, now a teenager herself, found out the hard way. You see, Meadow's father was Brian O'Conner of *Fast and Furious* fame on screen. But in real life, Paul Walker was her dad, and the Porsche that he was riding in on November 13, 2013, was not on the set of the next sequence of the famous franchise in which he starred. The skid marks at the smoke-filled crash site were not a testament to Hollywood's finest stage directors and stuntmen either. That day, this joy ride would be his last, as Meadow's dad paid the ultimate price of living by the very message these movies has spread around the world. Paul Walker died in that crash, and his charred remains must become a grave warning to us all: Rebellion is a bummer.

PUT IT TO WORK

- **To what are your children listening?** To what sites do they subscribe? The messaging from media, Facebook, or behind such blockbusters as *Fast and Furious* will have a deep effect on your children over time. Depending on the age of your children, consider well the best way and time to open up this conversation. Listen without being judgmental, with an ear to learn.

- **If your kids are teenagers, talk to them about the "teen scene."** What are their peers' attitudes about sex? Has anyone ever offered them drugs? Is it "easy" to get them? Is use common among their peers? What do they know about gang activity?

- **Did you struggle through a rebellious phase when you were a teenager?** Is this something you can use as a vulnerable moment to build a bridge to them and then share valuable lessons you learned as a result?

- Re-read the section, "What's a Parent to do?" **Jot down your own thoughts about any of the seven suggestions raised here** which seem most relevant to you right now.

Chapter Twelve

BREAKING FREE FROM ENTITLEMENT

If this country is ever demoralized, it will come from trying to live without work.[54]

— ABRAHAM LINCOLN

We need a refresher course in responsibility. The lead article read: "College student blames parents after she blew $90G college fund." You read it right. She blew the money, but in her mind it was her parents' fault. When asked how her parents were to blame for her spending huge amounts of money on clothes, spring break, and a European vacation, she reasoned: "Maybe they should have taught me how to budget a little better."

While it is undoubtedly true that parents should teach their children how to budget money and teaching the values that undergird a sense of responsibility are the duty of parents, what we see here is symptomatic of something deeper than parental neglect. In reality, there has been such a broad shift in perspective from one generation to another that many parents have been caught unaware and, therefore, are unprepared to face the challenges this breech has created. It is as though the gas gauge on our car unknowingly broke, so we just kept driving on down the highway only to grind to a sputtering halt in the middle of nowhere, leaving us desperate and confused that this thing that had always worked before has so miserably let us down. So what is it that has "broken" since we were young?

IS SOMETHING BROKEN?

Okay, *broken* may be too strong a word here. But that is the way it feels. The truth is, there is such a wide gap between the way children think now and the way we as adults were raised to think that it's easy to feel like something has just suddenly stopped working. One of the great ironies of the day in which we live is that, despite advances in so many ways and greater opportunities, young people are more dependent upon parents, governments, and handouts than at any time in modern history. So how did we get here?

Our forefathers took pride in pulling themselves up by their "own bootstraps." Many were pioneers and trailblazers. They overcame hardships and faced untold sufferings to stake their claims, whether on the frontiers of America's West or as struggling immigrant communities who came to the shores of New York and Los Angeles, Southern Europe, or Southeast Asia with not much more than the shirts on their backs. My own parents walked three miles to school in blizzards and snow drifts that were three feet high; but many children these days have come to expect a ride to school, to their friends' houses, and to their tuition centers —rain or shine. This is not a criticism or judgment against young people in our day. I only mean to highlight how wide the gap is. Unless we know what it looks like, and what has caused it, laboring to close it without mutual understanding can lead us down paths of discouragement, tension, and mistrust.

First, it is vital that you realize you are not alone. This is a cultural phenomenon that affects us all, young and old, and must be confronted shoulder to shoulder. Children should consider the effect this has had upon parents. Parents should appreciate that the easier path children have taken is not of their own choosing. Many feel alienated, disoriented, or overwhelmed due to the rapid changes that have occurred all around us.

Consider that I did not take my first flight until I was twenty-three years of age. My granddaughter flew twenty-three times while she was still in her mother's womb! The pace and scale of social transformation has no comparison at any place or time in history. This has created a shift of seismic proportions in the way parents and children see the world.

For children to turn and blame their parents for this shift, or for parents to say it is their children's fault, is about as profitable as two people who have survived a devastating earthquake to declare, "This whole mess is your fault!" Rather than casting blame, parents and children have to figure out a way to navigate through the debris the shakings have caused and find a way to reconstruct together. We must believe that bridges can be built and the chasm closed.

THE ME ME ME GENERATION

Many attempts have been made to describe the reasons for this gap. Surveys have been quite revealing. *Time* magazine's cover from May 20, 2013, was titled, "The Me Me Me Generation" with "Millennials are lazy, entitled narcissists who still live with their parents" as its subtitle. Time states that 58 percent of Millennials call themselves "entitled," and more than 70 percent of them admit to being "selfish." Sounds like quite an indictment![55]

Also known as Generation Y (Gen Yers), Millennials is the term used to describe the people who were born between the years 1980 and the early 2000s. While there are some positive traits that are also associated with this generation, including confidence and tolerance (Twenge, Generation Me), the fact that many from this time period have not had to struggle to make ends meet in the same way that their parents have has given them a skewed view of how the things we enjoy have been obtained. While not all of them will binge ninety thousand dollars over a college semester, the ingredients are there for all Gen Yers to guiltlessly partake of pleasures at the expense of their parents. When my daughter was six, she asked me to buy something for her and I told her that I did not have enough money, she innocently told me, "But Dad, just use that [credit] card!" The danger is that, when we think their innocence should be gone at age sixteen or twenty-two, they may still thinking, "But Dad, just use that card!"

The man who spends ten years to plant and nurture fruit trees naturally has a different appreciation for the apples harvested than the man who places a dollar on the counter to buy *one*. David Foster Wallace in his book *The Pale King* puts it in terms of perception: "We think ourselves now as eaters of the pie instead of makers of the pie."[56] Once one's identity has shifted from "I make pies" to "I eat pies," it is very, very difficult to return. If this trend continues, if we only have pie eaters and no pie makers, then there comes a time when there are no more pie eaters either! Margaret Thatcher had a witty way of describing this conundrum: "The problem with socialism is that you eventually run out of other people's money!"[57]

WHAT DOES ENTITLEMENT MEAN?

There are three types of entitlement. They are:

A Sense of Entitlement: an unrealistic, unmerited or inappropriate expectation of favorable living conditions and favorable treatment at the hands of others. Boiling this down, the person who has a sense of entitlement *feels that he is owed something* even though nothing has essentially been done to deserve it.

The Entitlement Generation: the group born between 1980 and 2000 who believe they are owed certain rights and benefits without further justification. Also known as Millennials or Generation Y (Gen Yers).

A Culture of Entitlement: suggests that many people now have highly unreasonable expectations about what they are entitled to. This results when the majority of people live with a sense of entitlement, thereby making it difficult, and counter-cultural, to live otherwise.

How can we know entitlement has become lodged in the psyche of this generation? For one thing, it wasn't so very long ago that people who received government handouts felt stigmatized and battled a sense of shame in doing so.[58] Not anymore. Consider too the following trends:

- Statistically there have never been more people on welfare in the U.S. (nearly 25 percent, including 38 percent of children). The trends are also the same in Canada and most of Europe.

- Food Stamp recipients in the U.S. increased 70 percent during the years of President Obama's administration.

- The number of Millennials living with their parents is higher now than it has ever been since these statistics were kept, and increases every year.

- This is the generation of the "selfie," of a fixation with self-portraits posted on Facebook and Instagram. It has been called a *generation of narcissists.*

- As "unmerited expectations of favorable living conditions and favorable treatment" has risen, so has per person debt. There are five times more families that have filed for bankruptcy now than in 1980.[59]

Although these statistics are taken from Western sources, the symptoms that have given rise to this tension are a worldwide phenomenon. Anthropologists now speak of a "global youth culture" of shared values, heroes, and topics created by the social media. The rapid growth of economies in Asia, for instance, has caused a psychological rift between the generation that sacrificed greatly in order to create wealth and their children who are the beneficiaries of their struggles. From 1983 to 2017, China's per capita income went from one hundred U.S. dollars per year to twelve thousand U.S. dollars per year.[60] Talk about a difference in perspective between generations!

Of the nations that have the highest household debt, nine of the top fifteen are from Asia.[61] Asian children in this generation are also more pandered to than their parents' generation; they are generally more coddled and, therefore, perplexed when called upon to bear real responsibility. Without realizing it, some of Asia's Tiger Moms have raised Panda Kids. How is it possible *not* to feel entitled in Asia? Birth rates are so low, and the elderly are now living so much longer, that often there is one child to two parents, and four grandparents, not including maids, all heaping their attention and lavishing gifts upon their young.

PARENTS' ROLES

Wise parents from both East and West recognize these social trends and take measures to prepare their children to face the world as responsible adults. We cannot assume that all our children are going to wake up with an epiphany about stewardship, or accountability, or fiscal restraint when they graduate from college. There is a reason why Millennials are returning to stay with their parents in striking numbers. We have sheltered them. We have given into their demands. We have indulged them. We have not required of them the same things that were required of us; rather, we have acquiesced and given to them, on the proverbial silver platter, things for which there should have been a demand, a proven trust, or reasonable conditions.

It may be countercultural, but we should not have rewarded them just because they participated in something. When mommies were crying, "If my Johnny doesn't get a prize, he will feel hurt," we should have told them that Johnny would have been better served by witnessing that, in the real world, hard work, achievement, and creativity are recognized and rewarded. And Johnny's mom should have understood that it was okay for him to feel let down, as it can both serve as a motivation for him to work harder next time, as well as give him a vital lesson about life.

TRAINING AND PREPARATION

Astronauts are prepared through rigorous training to withstand life in space or zero gravity. Marines are prepared by extreme means in order to make them capable of surviving on the front lines of battle. What "spacesuits" have we provided for our children to withstand the rigors of the workforce? What have we armed them with to fight in the trenches of the complex and often corrupt marketplaces of the world? God forbid that we cave in to them when they say the spacesuits are too cumbersome, so we give them tweed suits instead. And I would hate to think of what would happen to our "Marine" sons and daughters sent to war having learned all their tactics in a paint ball park or, worse yet, a video game!

Parents would do well to learn some simple lessons of these realities revealed to us in the animal world. An ancient proverb speaks plainly about some of life's basic lessons:

"Go to the ant, you sluggard, consider its ways and be wise!" (This speaks of diligence.)

"It has no commander, no overseer or ruler." (This speaks of self-reliance, and responsibility.)

"Yet it stores its provisions in summer and gathers its food in harvest." (This speaks of planning, and saving for the future.)

Or how about the example of one of the most beautiful of Nature's creatures? The butterfly begins life as a caterpillar, a wormlike larva spinning a cocoon. The larva remains hidden within the cocoon as it undergoes metamorphosis. When it's time for the butterfly to emerge, it must struggle and fight its way out of the cocoon. We are tempted to help by tearing open the cocoon, but that's the worst thing we could do. The struggle is what makes it strong, enabling it to fly. Have many of us foolishly torn open the "cocoons" of our children, imagining that we were helping them when in fact we were harming them instead?

Fortunately, many parents know enough not to tear open the cocoons of their children. Likewise, many children also exhibit "ant-like" characteristics. Just because there has been a massive sociological and cultural shift that has given rise to this sense of entitlement doesn't mean that all have succumbed, or that you will of necessity fall into the *me me me* web. The following story shows us that there is still a lot of good out there! Meredith, who is studying for her Ph.D., is certainly not bound by a sense of entitlement:

———

I had just graduated high school, and I was accepted to my top choice college, with a great financial aid package. I was on top of the world, and I was proud. I had attended a very competitive high school, so I felt good to say that I would be attending this prestigious school, that is, until I got a call from the university two weeks before orientation: "Hi, I'm from the finance department. I'm reaching out to let you know that you won't be able to attend orientation if your balance of $5,000 isn't paid." I thought surely this was a mistake since I had already paid for the semester with hard-earned money. It wasn't.

Growing up, I knew paying for my education would be my responsibility, and so I worked for it. I got my first job when I was 14. My financial aid package changed because my sister was no longer a dependent, and the government assumed my parents could then afford to help me more. The decrease in financial aid of $5,000 less each semester meant $10,000 more in loans, per year! I was already taking on more student loans than I was comfortable with, so I chose not to a attend the college of my dreams. An opportunity opened up for me (an aspiring historian) to get an internship at a museum with its archivist. I worked a retail job to save up and waited to see what door would open up for me.

I decided to go to another school that was my "safety net." It was much more affordable, but even then it was still just beyond my ability to pay. When I shared my hopes with my parents over Christmas, they did something that literally changed my life. They supported my dreams. They promised to help pay $2,000 every semester to help me go to school! This made my dream of an education attainable. I still had to work 70 hours a week during the summers, and 20 hours a week during the school year, to be able to afford my education. And I still have loans. But I am so grateful for my parents' sacrifice. It was completely unexpected. As the last of four children, I was the only one to get financial help to go to school. My parents reasoned that since the government wasn't helping me, they would make the extra effort.

I valued my education so much more because I had to really work for it. I took responsibility. I wasn't sure what I would do after graduation, so I did a variety of things, with excellence, knowing this would be most advantageous for me. I studied hard and got good grades. I was the president of a couple clubs like Model United Nations and the History Club. I became an Resident Advisor and served on the University Discipline Board. More importantly, I knew I would need a network of professors and staff who supported me, for letters of recommendation, etc. These grades, activities, and letters from professors were the basis for scholarships I received which paid completely for my master's program.

Now, as I'm applying to get my Ph.D., I am so thankful for my parents. First, they made my education attainable, but, more importantly, they taught me the value of my education, and they supported my dreams. I think there's a balance to "entitlement." On the one hand, I felt so alone as I looked at the dollar sign of my dreams. I simply could not have done it without their help. On the other hand, although they helped me, at the end of the day it wasn't their dream for my life; it was mine. I had to take responsibility for realizing my own dream, but without the financial and emotional support of my parents, I would not be where I am today.

CHORES

The values and habits that help make children successful as adults must be taught to them from the beginning. Every week my parents would make a chart of chores for me and my three brothers to do: Take out the trash, do the dishes, vacuum, mop, dust, make our beds, pick up our rooms, etc. Only when we had done all of the things that were assigned to us on any given week would we be given a financial reward or an allowance.

Pick up any parenting magazine or book, and the messages on this topic are consistent: Assigning chores works. Marty Rossmann, associate professor of family education at the University of Minnesota, is considered an expert on the impact of chores on the development of children. He says, "The best predictor of young adults' success in their mid-twenties was that they participated in household tasks" when they were young.[62] He recommends starting early, when they are three or four. The benefits are many, and include:

- It teaches the importance of giving back to parents, of being contributors to the household and not just beneficiaries.

- It equips them with skills that help them to live independently as adults.

- It teaches them the importance of performing an assigned task in a timely manner.

- It shows them the value of keeping work and living spaces uncluttered and organized.

- Some tasks are performed with others, teaching the value of teamwork.

- It is a means of reducing overindulgence and of becoming disciplined.

Though not all experts agree on whether an allowance should be given for basic chores, or for "jobs," the principle is that there should be a reward for work done well. In some cases, this involves money. This helps children to manage money wisely from a young age and learn of the value that is connected with money.

When our son Daniel was eleven and started a "business"

engaging a couple classmates and his sister in the sale of candy to his classmates, it translated to the perfect opportunity to teach him a life lesson about how to save his money, and generally be fiscally responsible. When I told him that I opened my first bank account to save money from a newspaper delivery job that I had when I was his age, he was suddenly motivated to do the same. The look on his face when he discovered that he could open a four-figure bank account was priceless! Whether Daniel goes on to start his own company some day remains to be seen, but there are valuable lessons here about creativity and stewardship and thrift that will stick with him for a lifetime.

A MESSAGE TO OUR CHILDREN

Given the influence of entitlement upon your generation, and upon culture as a whole, breaking free from its entanglements is going to take extra effort, much patience, and making hard choices. If you simply follow the crowds, you may find yourself ill-prepared to hold a job, or raise a family. If you are like so many of your peers, your cravings for gadgets or certain brands of cars or clothes, or entertainment, will come back to haunt you because you will spend beyond your means and wind up crumbling under the weight of preventable debt.

As the material world around you screams for your attention, and as its pickpockets target you through ads, fashions, or celebrity lifestyles, you are going to have to guard yourself from its tentacles. Otherwise, your "Precious" which you thought you owned will soon own you. Be warned. The road to Mordor is a treacherous one![63]

Consider well these wise words of G.K. Chesterton: "There are two ways to get enough. One is to continue to accumulate more and more. The other is to desire less."[64]

Something that is good for you to learn about your parents is that they are influenced by some very unhealthy cultural forces as well. Even though it has proven to be a formula for disaster, over and over again, many will feel compelled to indulge you (give you what you want). Their friends do it, their colleagues do it, and perhaps they were indulged themselves. Or, they may have felt deprived, in which case they likely hear a little voice inside them saying, "It was *so bad* for you growing up that you must *never* let this happen to your own children."

That's right, either way there is a strong possibility you will be sheltered and provided for lavishly. You will likely have way more toys than you can play with, and you will also very likely not be asked to work for or earn the things that will be given to you. This despite the wisdom of an adage developed through the ages: "Give a man a fish, you feed him for a day. Teach a man to fish, you feed him for a lifetime."[65]

The point here is that both parents and children alike must work to break a bad cycle. You, too, have to decide to be a fish catcher, and not just a fish eater.

So, this is my suggestion: Don't pressure your parents to get all these things for you. Don't make them feel guilty when you see your friends have the latest "toy" and you don't. This is one thing that you must not be passive about. The entitlement bug is trying to bite you! The walls of materialism are closing in on you from every side seeking to form you in its image. Are you going to sit back and let it? Or will you go to the ant and be wise.

When you are tempted to believe that you deserve this or that, or to be treated in this special way or that, or that a free lunch is the best lunch, please consider: Life in the real world does not work this way. Surveys have uncovered that many students today openly admit their goal is to succeed with the least amount of effort. You might as well say you are going to attempt to ride a bike without wheels! Consider this quote from best-selling author Larry Winget:

> Taking responsibility is the most critical step toward success that you will ever make in anything you undertake, either personally or professionally. The ability to take responsibility for everything you are, everything you do and everything you have is also the biggest challenge you will ever face in your life.[66]

We *go* to school, *get* a job, *have* a dream, but we *take* responsibility. I got my first job as a paper boy when I was ten. I would get up at five in the morning to collect my papers and have them distributed in time to take the bus to school. With the money I earned, I bought a bicycle. I could do my route quicker, and I did not need to get up as early. This gave me a deep sense of satisfaction and accomplishment. I am so thankful that my parents taught me the value of taking responsibility when I was young, as it has served me well over a lifetime. I paid for and worked my way through college. I paid off my student loans two years after I graduated, so I rid myself as quickly as possible of the debts that encumber so many. Who out there could argue that I was not being blessed?

THE VALUE OF WORK

Kay Wills Wyma in her book, *Cleaning House: A Mom's Twelve-Month Experiment to Rid Her Home of Youth Entitlement*, writes:

> Instead of communicating "I love you, so let me make life easy for you," I decided that my message needed to be something more along these lines: "I love you. I believe in you. I know what you're capable of. So I'm going to make you work."[67]

People used to work hard without recognition. But society has turned this concept around on its head, so that people are being given recognition and "rewarded" even when they don't work hard. The best practice is to have both. People need to work hard, *and* they should be praised for it. Work is both a source of identity and a wellspring of dignity. Whereas welfare systems may start as a safety net for those stuck in troubled times or who fall upon hardships, over time they betray the intentions of those who craft them and tend to prop up laziness and complacency. This gives rise to a news headlines I read last week, "Feeding a 'Why Work' Mindset?"[68] It seems President Lincoln was more than a great president, he was a kind of a prophet too when he said 160 years ago: "If this country is ever demoralized, it will come from trying to live without work."[69]

In 1981, the *American Journal of Psychiatry* completed

comprehensive research on the importance of work. The director of the study, George Valliant, reported:

> The single biggest predictor of adult mental health was "the capacity to work learned in childhood"—in other words, the development of a work ethic.[70]

Men who Valliant described as "competent and industrious at age 14"—men who had developed a work ethic during the Industry Stage of human development—were twice as likely to have warm relationships, five times more likely to have well-paying jobs and 16 times less likely to have suffered significant unemployment.

He further concluded there is a "direct, positively correlative relationship between combating an attitude of entitlement in your child's youth and his or her happiness and success later in life."[71]

CONCLUSION

It is as though a courtroom has been adjourned. Mounds of evidence have been presented. Key witnesses, young and old, journalists, psychiatrists, philosophers have been called. Meanwhile, we see many who have been unwittingly bound by chains of debt, laziness, or overindulgence. Before the gavel falls, there is yet time to stand firm and state: "My destiny is not with those who languish in the prisons that have closed its doors on so many from my generation. Judge, I will not be a victim, nor will I cast blame on others. Today, I make my stand; *I will be free from entitlement!*"

I come from a long line of pie makers. Pecan pies. Strawberry Rhubarb pies. Apple pies. My wife's pumpkin pies are historic. If I want my grandkids to enjoy pies, we're going to have to teach our own sons and daughters not just to eat them but to make them, too. I'd much prefer to settle this matter out of court. Let's take this battle back to our kitchens. Let's teach the next generation about the values of work and of being fiscally responsible from their youth. Let's show them the way of the ant. We can put a finger in this cultural levee. Come on, Parents. This is a battle we do not want to lose.

PUT IT TO WORK

- I mention "a shift of seismic proportions in the way parents and children see the world." In a relaxed atmosphere free from criticism, but to increase mutual understanding, **talk about some of these differences**.

- **Have an honest discussion with your spouse about ways you may have contributed to an entitlement mentality in your kids.** Have you sheltered them? Have you given in to their demands or indulged them? What are some of the ways you can encourage your children in the short- and long-term to bear responsibility? The struggle of the larvae in the cocoon strengthens it to be able to fly when it emerges. What things can you do assure that you are not tearing open the "cocoons" of your children?

- Marty Rossman said that the best predictor of success as adults is whether or not children participated in chores or household tasks as they were growing up. **Do you incorporate chores into your children's weekly routine?**

- **Talk to your kids about the ill effects of debt to which many of their generation have fallen prey.** If they don't already have a bank account to start their own savings, as you walk them through this, it is a great time to talk about not only staying free from debt, but of the sense of fulfillment one has in growing one's wealth.

- Meredith writes, "I valued my education so much more because I had to really work for it." **Read her story, and talk together with your kids about her view** that "there's a balance to 'entitlement.'"

Chapter Thirteen

I FORGIVE YOU

If I could convince the patients in psychiatric hospitals
that their sins were forgiven, 75 percent of them
could walk out the next day![72]

— KARL MENNINGER, PSYCHIATRIST

*S*orry. It's the longest five-letter-word in the English language. Among the 170,000 words in the *Oxford Dictionary,* it also has a very unique status: *Sorry* is the word we most like to hear, and at the same time the word we find most difficult to say. To unlock the mystery behind the word, we have to explore regions with astronomic resolve and wonder. We have to look into the human heart.

In one sense, I don't have to look far—six to eight inches to be exact. I know where it is, and I wear a watch that tells me how many times it beats every minute, resting or running, throughout the day. Understanding this organ should not be that difficult, right? Well, yes, except for the fact that the things in these hearts of ours, on the one hand, can invoke the highest heights of reverence when a fellow sojourner impresses by the most honorable and sacrificial of deeds, and in the next minute embarrass us to shame by the frailty and selfishness of another.

People of all backgrounds, every age, irrespective of race, economic condition, or religion, all face a common foe: offense. Jesus once said, "Woe to the world because of offenses!"[73] Hearts get wounded, stepped on. It is impossible to escape being wronged. The question is not if, but when. Which leads to the next question: What? What am I going to do about it? Will I reconcile, or will I avoid? Will it be fight or flight? Will I flow or flee? Will I build a wall or cross a bridge? The good news is that we also all have a common friend: choice. We can choose to forgive.

CHOOSING TO FORGIVE

Forgiving is one of the most difficult yet important lessons you will ever learn. Whether you are eight or eighty years of age, you will experience times when people will let you down. You will be misunderstood, neglected, or taken advantage of—guaranteed. It hurts, doesn't it! If you scrape your knee, you take time to put antiseptic and a bandaid on the wound to guard against infection. How much more do we need to heal the wounds on our hearts! But how? Is there a medicine that is effective?

Sadly, many people go through life not realizing there is a medicine for such wounds. Their emotional wounds turn into nasty scars. The heart that has been hurt can devise personality-altering defenses to avoid the pain again. Bitterness festers. Friendships can be ruined. Marriages paralyzed. Office spaces, classrooms, neighborhoods become like war zones. Despite the good news that we all have the power to choose to forgive, the bad news is that it is never easy to forgive others when they have either intentionally or accidentally scandalized you. It takes courage.

Although everyone likes to be forgiven, it doesn't mean everyone is willing to forgive. It also is no assurance that once forgiveness is offered that it will accepted. But according to psychologist and author Larry Phillip Nims, giving *and* receiving forgiveness is a key to physical and psychological health. Dr. Nims, who lists twelve ways that unforgiveness negatively affects us, says: "I am convinced that unforgiveness and related attitudes of resentment and bitterness are among the deadliest dynamics in the human psyche."[74]

While forgiveness is indispensable in all types of relationships—among neighbors, friends, classmates, or colleagues—there is no place where forgiveness needs to be practiced more than at home. Why? Because whenever an offense lingers, just being around the other person can be anything from uncomfortable to intolerable! You can change your job, or seek out other friendships, but you cannot change your family.

FAMILY CULTURE

The people with whom you are most likely to have conflict

are the people with whom you have the most contact. If a passerby treats you rudely, you are not likely to lose sleep over it. But if you have a strong disagreement with one who sits across from you at the dinner table every night, you can't simply ignore it. The closer the ties, the greater the need to learn to let go, to extend grace, and to make peace. The family who practices forgiveness is a family who can live in the present rather than sorrowfully looking over the shoulder at yesterday. The atmosphere is cleared of smoke, the closets of skeletons, and the floors of debris. Forgiveness makes a house into a home.

Chinese will often hang these four characters—出入平安 —over the entrance of their homes (especially at New Year), blessing all who enter, and all who leave, with peace. More than a slogan or annual tradition, I have determined that our home will be a haven of peace, to family first, and then to all who enter. I wish it was as easy as posting an auspicious sign; peace is something for which we must contend, however. I have also realized that creating this culture begins with me. If I am harboring grudges, I cannot expect others to take the high road and extend an olive branch. Although in many cultures it is virtually unheard of for a father to ask forgiveness, as though it is a sign of weakness, I unabashedly would call this a harmful lie! *Far from being weak, leadership is stepping forward to confess a wrong done or sorrow for painful words spoken in anger.* If you are a parent, it is never too late to do the right thing. Be an example, and start today.

People who go through life with unresolved conflict do so to their own peril. As painful as bitter exchanges can be among friends, at least you get to choose your friends! Not so with family. Husbands and wives are bound by lifelong commitments. You don't get to choose your brothers and sisters, and you can't decide that you would rather have someone else for your parents, or pass your children on to someone else to deal with.

Whether you are parent or child, older sibling or younger sibling, don't make the grave mistake of waiting for someone else to take the first step to reconcile. I have known of cases when children have taken the first steps towards healing a breech in a relationship with parents, confessing disrespect, disregard, or rebellion that led to a breakdown in a healthy relationship with their mom or dad, or both. Forgiveness not only heals *me*; it heals *us*.

A DAUGHTER'S LETTER TO DAD

Marianne Williamson is an author who has written a lot on the topic of forgiveness. She writes, *"The practice of forgiveness is our most important contribution to the healing of the world."*[75] This is a sentiment Jeh Sie would say applies to her very personally as she shares her story about the day she and her father, Mr. Tan Tek Seng, who now chairs the organization Family First Malaysia, found strength to forgive each other:

————

When I was growing up, I used to wish that my dad would be more like the American dream dad who we watched on TV. I wanted a dad who regularly would gather the family around for talks, who brought his daughters out for date nights, who made time to sit and watch movies with us. I wanted my dad to listen, to say sorry when he had made a mistake or been too harsh. I wanted a perfect dad.

Dad was a busy businessman. He was out most nights at functions and meetings. In his mind, being a good dad meant providing for the physical needs of his children. In his mind, he thought it was the mother's job to bring up the children and see to their emotional needs.

Sure, Dad did give us lots of hugs and kisses. He provided well for us. But what I wanted most from him during those years was quality time and his undivided attention.

Some time in my teenage years, resentment started building up in my heart. Dad was constantly on the phone when we were supposed to be spending "quality family time" during holidays. He did not listen and kept getting distracted halfway through conversations we were having. He was always too busy. He never said sorry.

With bitterness and unforgiveness gnawing away at my heart, it was difficult to see the blessings. All I could see was what my dad did not do, how he had wronged me. This even began to have an effect on my spiritual life. So I decided I needed to reconcile with my earthly dad. Even though it was quite humbling to make the first move, the breakthrough came when I wrote my dad a letter. This was what I wrote in my diary that day: "I reconciled with my Dad. ☺ He made me really mad at first as he 'lectured' me (in some sense, trying to justify himself). But when I prayed [with him], he cried. Thank You, Lord, that You've helped us forgive each other and may You cement this relationship. Build us up as father-daughter in Your love, Lord."

That was the first time I saw my dad cry. He also said, "Sorry." It was a huge step for an Asian dad to apologize and admit that he had wronged his child. It was certainly a pivotal moment in our relationship.

Being able to forgive led me on to a new appreciation for my dad. Although he still has his shortcomings, I now know he is a good dad. He loves us but shows it through his predominant love language which is "acts of service." He loves to tend to our gardens and clean down hard to reach areas when he comes to visit our homes now that we've all grown up. Dad has remained faithful to my mother, and they model what a loving and godly marriage should be like. Dad prays for us and supports the decisions we have to make in life. When I went off to university, Dad even made the effort to accompany me on the plane and made sure I settled in well. That was a special week of bonding between us.

Over the years, I realize that I have changed. I have forgiven my dad and can actually laugh over what I used to resent or get irritated by. Now that I am a parent myself, I have come to value and understand the huge responsibility Dad and Mom had in raising three children while juggling their own business. My dad is not perfect, but none of us are, and that's okay.

———

FORGIVENESS IS GOOD FOR YOU!

According to a survey by the nonprofit Fetzer Institute, 62 percent of American adults say they need more forgiveness in their personal lives.[76] But unlike other "illnesses," people are not lining up at the local clinic to get cured! Bitterness and resentment are not on the list of the Center for Disease Control. And though it can be highly contagious, you will not find unforgiveness on any list of infectious diseases in medical journals, neither does your local pharmacy sell any prescriptions or even offer any over-the-counter drugs which can heal acrimony between family and friends.

Comparing unforgiveness to disease is not simply an illustration. This subject is no longer confined to the realm of psychiatry; it has increasingly found its way into the field of medicine where its longterm physical effects on people is now well documented. Consider, for instance, this article by Dr. Karen Swartz of Johns Hopkins, "Forgiveness: Your Health Depends On It":

Whether it's a simple spat with your spouse or long-held resentment toward a family member or friend, unresolved conflict can go deeper than you may realize—it may be affecting your physical health. The good news: Studies have found that the act of forgiveness can reap huge rewards for your health, lowering the risk of heart attack; improving cholesterol levels and sleep; and reducing pain, blood pressure, and levels of anxiety, depression and stress. And research points to an increase in the forgiveness-health connection as you age.[77]

Dr. Swartz goes on to say that holding on to unforgiveness can produce a state of chronic anger which in turn "increases the risk of depression, heart disease, and diabetes, among other conditions." As a medical professional, she then goes on to recommend making forgiveness an integral part of our lives.[78] It makes relational, emotional, and physical sense.

A SILENT KILLER

As horrible as the tragedy of Nagasaki and Hiroshima was, a nuclear bomb has only ever been dropped once on the planet in war in the history of the world. While we commemorate this day and highlight its effects as a deterrent, as we should, we have no such reminder for the meltdowns that have littered the pages of history due to the effects of unforgiveness. In this sense, and in contrast to a bomb, it is a silent killer, like a parasite that grows inside the host, consuming from the inside out. There are no fallout shelters to which people run to escape, as in the case of the impending doom of nuclear destruction. And yet, like the lingering effects of radiation, unforgiveness is deadly.

In one of the most poignant and iconic images taken from Western classics, the main character in *Pilgrim's Progress* carried a heavy and intolerable load he referred to as "my burden" throughout the book. Painful as it was ("this burden that is upon my back will sink me lower than the grave"), try as he may, he simply could not rid himself of this grievous menace. Though he wished to go faster along his journey, his "burden" mired him and provoked him to despondency. Its weight so pressed upon him, that he felt it impossible to enjoy life as he once had. He relentlessly sought relief, begging all those he encountered along his weary way. That is until at last, by forgiveness, "his burden loosed from off his shoulders, and fell from off his back, and began to tumble, and so continued to do, till it came to the mouth of the sepulcher, where it fell in, and I saw it no more."[79]

YOU CAN DO IT!

You don't have to carry your burden either. If Corrie Ten Boom could forgive the cruelty of the prison guards who tortured and maimed the innocent millions who passed through the concentration camps during the heinous times of Nazi Germany, you can muster up the courage to say sorry to your spouse, or forgive that person at school, or work.

When I read Corrie's story, *The Hiding Place*, to my three youngest kids last year, every night they nestled around me to listen as the tale of how this humble Dutch watchmaker's Haarlem home had become a sanctuary for Jews who had been marked for extermination by Hitler. While eight hundred people were saved through the Ten Boom's selfless resistance, their family was not so fortunate. They were caught and sent to the very same camps from which they were saving others. Blind cruelty, humiliation, and intense suffering were their rewards for kindness and unconditional mercy.

While many if not most of the people who lived through these horrors were marred for life, Corrie, like Pilgrim, had managed to rid herself of Burden's tortuous effects, witnessing it tumble down the mountain of her past and swallowed by the grave below forever. Rather than wallowing in miry memories, she turned mourning into message, and until the age of eighty-six traveled to more than fifty countries to bring hope to people who needlessly were hanging on to transgressions big and small that had been done against them.

During her travels, she related the day she came face to face with the man who in the camps had become the very personification of evil. He approached her in Munich, offered her his hand in greeting, and told her how much he appreciated her message, affirming God had washed away his sins. She struggled inside:

> Even as the angry, vengeful thoughts boiled through me, I saw the sin of them. Jesus Christ had died for this man; was I going to ask for more? I tried to smile, I struggled to raise my hand. I could not. I felt nothing, not the slightest spark of warmth or charity. And so again I breathed a silent prayer. Jesus, I prayed, I cannot forgive him. Give me Your forgiveness.
>
> As I took his hand the most incredible thing happened. From my shoulder along my arm and through my hand a current seemed to pass from me to him, while into my heart sprang a love for this stranger that almost overwhelmed me. And so I discovered that it is not on our forgiveness any more than on our goodness that the world's healing hinges, but on His. When He tells us to love our enemies, He gives, along with the command, the love itself.[80]

Corrie chose to forgive when she had a thousand reasons not to. Her life message is a powerful injunction to us all, that regardless of how we feel, mustering up the courage to forgive is the right thing to do.

A CROSS

Corrie is not the only one who has been moved to courageously extend forgiveness to others because of the example of Jesus on the cross. Consider the true story of Olympic athlete Louis Zamperini which is told in the book, *Unbroken*, and which was made into a major motion picture of the same name directed by Angelina Jolie. Louis, too, is a great and shining light to people who have wintered the most trying seasons of injustice only to find the warmth, bloom, and fragrance of a spring of hope dawning. The fact that he could return to the very Japanese World War 2 prison, where he and his fellow soldiers had been subject to the most inhuman treatment imaginable, and extend a hug and not a dagger to his captors is sure to leave you with renewed resolve not to keep a record of wrongs done to you, not even for another day.

Whether you are a Christian or not, a chapter about forgiveness would not be complete without mentioning the symbol which has been the single greatest inspiration for people to forgive in history. In life, Jesus' message about forgiveness was striking. When asked by his disciple Peter how many times he should forgive a brother who had sinned against him, Peter thought seven times was a good goal to shoot for. But Jesus answered, "I do not say to you up to seven times, but seventy times seven."[81] These giant words have stood the test of generation after generation, spanning cultures and classes, raising a standard while at the same time convincing us with unbridled wisdom that, in fact, we are all better off if we will only continuously walk in this grace.

It was in his death, however, that the message of forgiveness hits us like the nails that clamped him to the cross. Having performed good, taught kindness, and exemplified the highest ethical values in life, he had been groundlessly tried and sentenced to death by crucifixion, then flogged and tortured despicably in historically climactic fashion, as he was stripped naked and hung publicly upon a hill for all to see. Before his tormenters, the very soldiers who had ripped the skin off his back with whips, and two convicted criminals similarly impaled on his right hand and left, he cried out to God his Father that every last one of them, guilty as they were, should be completely, unconditionally forgiven.

CLOSING THOUGHTS ON FORGIVENESS

Finally, let me share some practical thoughts in closing about forgiveness.

- A common pitfall is we wait for the other party to initiate forgiveness. We often think that their fault is greater, and therefore he or she should be the one to raise the matter first. My suggestion? Get over it. Swallow your pride. *Go to your "brother" first,* offer sincere apologies for your own wrongs and shortcomings, and tell him or her you deeply

value your relationship and don't want anything
to stand in the way.

- When forgive is offered, *it must be received.* And
  don't just say, "Thank you," either. It may seem
  trivial, but there is power in the words, "I forgive
  you." You would not keep your hand at your side
  in response to an extended hand of welcome or
  blessing; neither should you keep your words
  inside. Forgiveness is always a two-way street. It
  must be given, and it must be received.

- *Be sincere.* The words and the act of forgiveness are
  important in and of themselves. In fact, there are
  times when you don't really *feel* like this is natural
  or easy to do. But as much as you can, make sure
  that you come to the place where your
  "forgiveness" is not just lip service. If you have
  time to prepare for the moment when you will sit
  down with the one(s) to whom you are being
  reconciled, as much as is possible, in your heart,
  settle the matter in all sincerity first.

- Sadly, there are cases when the other party refuses
  to be reconciled. Even when there is no real peace
  between you, make sure that you at least have
  peace *within* yourself. You cannot force your will
  upon another, but you can *leave your burden and
  move on.* Hope for another chance when the other
  party is ready, and seek opportunity without
  forcing your hope on him or her. At the end of the

day, some will not reconcile, but you can still be confident that you have done everything within your power to make it right.

- *Don't let the nuclear affects of unresolved conflict and strife steal joy and contentment from your family.* Over the years, I have witnessed homes that were threatened by the holocaust of broken relationships restored, turning away from a spiral of despair to stand upon a rock of security and stability. Upon the tree of unforgiveness hangs the fruits of anger, revenge, insomnia, criticism, manipulation, alienation, and violence. Cut it down, quickly! Plant in its place the tree of grace, whereupon the fruits of patience, kindness, gentleness, community, peace, and encouragement grow. I know it's hard to say, but decide today to say, "I forgive you," and make *sorry* not the hardest, but your favorite five-letter word.

It is fitting that a chapter on forgiveness is the capstone of the qualities I have written of in this book. In truth, parents and their children alike can improve in every other sheep, dog, and horse quality herein, but if they fail in the ultimate practice of forgiveness, an inherent frailty and poison will remain, which will have adverse effects on their relationships. Strangely, the word *unforgiveness* is underlined as I type, indicating this monstrous concept is not even found in this software's dictionary! Despite this enormous oversight, I hope and pray the words, "I forgive you," will be a regular part of your vocabulary.

The relationships Joyce and I have with our children are our richest treasure and our most lasting legacy. We've had to work hard to get to where we are, but the way that our sons and daughters of every age have responded to our efforts to instill in them the qualities we have shared with you here has reaped the most marvelous results. May it become your story and legacy as well. May each of your children grow up to be able to say, "I love you, Mom and Dad. And by the way, I LIKE you, too!"

PUT IT TO WORK

The best way to put the last chapter to work for you is to make sure that all the relationships in your household are not paralyzed by unforgiveness. Take the lead. This is what I suggest:

- **Re-read the section on "Family Culture."** Make your own commitment to a family culture where the atmosphere is "cleared of smoke, the closets of skeletons, and the floors of debris." Then re-read the section "Closing Thoughts on Forgiveness."

- **Plan a movie night and rent *Unbroken.*** Watch it together. Make sure you start early enough, and allow for some time following the movie to talk about the power of forgiveness.

- **Show leadership.** Humble yourself and confess your own shortcomings. You may want to apologize for painful words you spoke in anger or a wrong attitude you had.

- **Encourage all the other members of the household to be reconciled to each other.** Share your commitment to a new family culture.

- **And tell them you love them and like them, too. :)**

EPILOGUE

*J*eremy and Daniel had never played darts before. While on a family vacation, I found them in the hotel lobby where a board hung. They were giving it a try. Since our family had a dartboard when I was growing up, I decided I would show them a thing or two. When I hit dead center on my second shot, my boys were visibly impressed!

I realized this was an ideal opportunity for a teaching moment. "Boys," I said, "many people live their lives and never hit the bullseye. In fact, many aren't even sure what the target is. They are just shooting darts at the next thing that catches their attention. For me, the thrill of the game is hitting the bullseye. And when I think about my life and yours, I also want to know that we are hitting dead center of the target that is designed just for us."

A moment later, Daniel, who was eleven at the time, launched a dart that had a bent tip. It hit the board, but bounced off and fell to the ground.

"This speaks to me about character, boys," I said. "The person who is crooked will never succeed. You saw it. It was a good shot, but the dart fell to the ground in failure." Though it was a simple illustration, I think my dart hit the target of their hearts that day.

No parent wants to see his or her children "fall to the ground." And yet, many of us also don't have a clear vision of the target our children should be shooting at. In some cases, we haven't guarded their "tips" from becoming dull, rusty, or bent.

When I set out on this journey of writing a book, I identified these twelve qualities that Joyce and I have worked hard to instill in our seven children. Despite ups and downs, and a few bumps and bruises, it has reaped tremendous results for us. I can honestly say that, today, they not only love us as their mom and dad, but they like us, too!

When I hit the bullseye that day, it was probably 1 percent skill and 99 percent luck. When it comes to raising awesome kids, this is not something to leave to chance.

NOTES

1. Proverbs 31:27-29 (NET).
2. Judy Dutton, "How Swimming Saved Michael Phelps: An ADHD Story." *Attitude*. Accessed March 10, 2018. https://www.additudemag.com/michael-phelps-adhd-advice-from-the-olympians-mom/.
3. Zig Ziglar, "Zig Ziglar Quotes." *Brainy Quotes*. Accessed March 10, 2018. https://www.brainyquote.com/authors/zig_ziglar.
4. Charles Dickens, "Quote by Charles Dickens." *Quotery*. Accessed March 11, 2018. https://www.quotery.com/quotes/reflect-upon-your-present-blessings-of-which-every-man-has/.
5. Gregory W. Clayton, *Be A Better Dad Today*. (Ventura: Regal, 2012), 100.
6. A. A. Milne, "A. A. Milne: Quotes." *Goodreads*. Accessed March 18, 2018. https://www.goodreads.com/author/quotes/81466.A_A_Milne.

7. Booker T. Washington, "Booker T. Washington Quote." *Liberty-Tree*. Accessed March 18, 2018. http://quotes.liberty-tree.ca/quote_blog/Booker. T..Washington.Quote.4050.

8. Arthur Ward, "William Arthur Ward Quotes," *Brainy Quotes*. Accessed March 18, 2018. https://www.brainyquote.com/quotes/william_ arthur_ward_105516.

9. Corrie ten Boom, Elizabeth Sherrill, and John Sherill, *The Hiding Place* (Guideposts Associates, 1971).

10. Thomas Jefferson, "Honesty is the first chapter in the book of wisdom (Quotation)." *Monticello*. https://www.monticello.org/site/jefferson/honesty-first-chapter-book-wisdom-quotation.

11. George Washington Inn, "The Legend of the Cherry Tree," *George Washing Inn & Estate*. March 21, 2009. Accessed March 10, 2018. https://georgewashingtoninn.wordpress.com/2009/03/21/the-legend-of-the-cherry-tree/.

12. "What's so honest about Abe?" *"Life of a Remote Leader."* February 12, 2010. Accessed on March 26, 2018. https://jasonchristensen.wordpress.com/2010/02/12/honest-abe/.

13. Mark E. Steiner, *An Honest Calling: The Law Practice of Abraham Lincoln* (Northern Illinois University Press, 2009).

14. Turnitin, "Plagiarism: Facts & Stats." *p.org*. June 7, 2017. Accessed March 10, 2018. http://www.plagiarism.org/article/plagiarism-facts-and-stats.

15. *The Strait Times*, "Indian court bars hundreds of

student doctors over cheating on exams." February 13, 2017. Accessed March 14, 2018. http://www.straitstimes.com/asia/south-asia/indian-court-bars-hundreds-of-student-doctors-over-cheating-on-exams.

16. *South China Morning Post (International)*, "Why do Chinese students think it's OK to cheat?" June 14, 2016. Accessed March 18, 2018. http://www.straitstimes.com/asia/south-asia/indian-court-bars-hundreds-of-student-doctors-over-cheating-on-exams.

17. Chris Matthews, "Here's How Much Tax Cheats Cost the U.S. Government a Year" *Fortune*. April 29, 2016. Accessed March 21, 2018. http://fortune.com/2016/04/29/tax-evasion-cost/.

18. Proverbs 3:1-2 (NIV).

19. J. Karl Laney, *Marching Orders* (Victor, 1983), 50.

20. Anne Frank. *The Diary of a Young Girl* (New York: Bantam, 1993), 256.

21. Corrie ten Boom, Elizabeth Sherrill, and John Sherill, *The Hiding Place* (Guideposts Associates, 1971), 138.

22. Alexander Solzhenitsyn, "More Quotes by Alexander Solzhenitsyn," *Forbes Quotes*. Accessed on March 21, 2018. https://www.forbes.com/quotes/author/alexander-solzhenitsyn/.

23. Aristotle, "Aristotle Quote," *IZQuotes*. Accessed March 21, 2018. http://izquotes.com/quote/6857.

24. Exodus 20:12 (NKJV).

25. Larry Stockstill, "Honor," *Larry Stockstill*. Accessed

March 21, 2018. https://www.larrystockstill.com/
blog/honor.

26. Sandra Gibson, ATEC G5, "The code of honor;
     know it, embrace it," *U.S. Army*. Accessed March
     12, 2018. https://www.army.mil/article/98038/
     the_code_of_honor_know_it_embrace_it.

27. David Crouch. *The Birth of Nobility: Constructing
     Aristocracy in England and France 900-1300* (Harlow,
     UK: Pearson), 79.

28. American Adoption Congress, "Reform Myths,"
     American Adoption Congress. Accessed March 15,
     2018. https://www.americanadoptioncongress
     .org/reform_myths.php.

29. The affect of the Great Awakening on Western
     society was far-reaching. Crime rates were
     dramatically curbed. The status of women was
     raised, standards in education were elevated, and
     civility and courtesy replaced coarseness and
     confrontation in government and public
     discourse. Many have argued that it gave rise to a
     national consciousness and unity which were
     necessary components to the United States being
     formed as a sovereign nation. One of this
     grassroots movement's most celebrated
     achievements was the momentum which had
     gathered steam in America then spread to Great
     Britain (Jonathan Edwards had personally played a
     major role in igniting a fire in the heart of George
     Whitefield) and had a direct impact on legislation
     which abolished slavery in England and
     throughout the Commonwealth.

30. A.E. Winship, "Full text of 'Jukes-Edwards: A Study in Education and Heredity,'" *Internet Archive.* Accessed March 20, 2018. http://archive .org/stream/jukesedwards15623gut/15623.txt.

31. Master Oogway, "Master Oogway: Quotes: Quotable Quotes," *Goodreads.* Accessed on March 21, 2018. https://www.goodreads.com/quotes/ 2212546-yesterday-is-history-tomorrow-is-a-mystery-and-today-is.

32. Much has been written in recent years about right and left brain differences. All our educational systems are "left brain" orientated. When we as parents unlock the right-brain potential of our kids, a whole new and exciting world is opened up to them. See https://www.psychologytoday.com/ blog/not-born-yesterday/201210/are-you-left-or-right-brain-dominant.

33. 1 Kings 10:5 (NKJV).

34. Proverbs 6:20-23 (NIV).

35. Fandom, "Kung Fu Panda," *Encyclopedia & Community: Kung Fu Panda Wiki.* Accessed March 21, 2018. http://kungfupanda.wikia.com/ wiki/Kung_Fu_Panda.

36. Obi-wan Kenobi is the master trainer of the famed Jedi fighters of the *Star Wars* films.

37. Gandalf is the creation of J. R. R. Tolkien of the famed *The Hobbit* and *The Lord of the Rings* trilogy and is indisputably the wisest person in "Middle Earth."

38. Louisa May Alcott, AZ Quotes. Accessed March

10, 2018. http://www.azquotes.com/quote/ 392287.

39. "Neglect and Other Problems Suffered by Elderly People in China," *Facts and Details*. Accessed March 19, 2018. http://factsanddetails.com/china/ cat4sub21/ entry-4461.html.

40. From *A Writer's Year—Fennel's Journal, No. 3.* "Fennel Hudson: Quotes: Quotable Quote," *Goodreads*. Accessed March 19, 2018. https://www.goodreads.com/quotes/7149581- mine-is-a-so-called-vintage-existence- anachronistic-living-made-all.

41. Theodor Reik, "Theodor Reik Quote," *IZQuotes*. Accessed March 19, 2018. http://izquotes.com/ quote/318828.

42. Constance Chuks Friday, "Quotes by Constance Chuks Friday," *Brainywords*. Accessed March 21, 2018. http://www.brainywords.com/quotes/view/ a/quotes-by-constance-chuks-friday-221115.html.

43. Psalm 1:1 (NKJV).

44. Richelle E. Goodrich, "Making Wishes Quotes," *Goodreads*. Accessed March 20, 2018. https:// www.goodreads.com/work/quotes/45430037- making-wishes?page=10.

45. John Steckroth, "Michigan teens charged in deadly I-75 rock throwing case have probably cause hearing," *ClickOnDetroit*. November 2, 2017. Accessed March 13, 2018. https://www.goodreads .com/work/quotes/45430037-making-wishes? page=10.

46. "Eiffel Tower, France," *UMass Boston*. Accessed

March 17, 2018. http://blogs.umb.edu/building
theworld/iconic-monuments/the-eiffel-tower-
france/.

47. Rick Warren, "Rebellion Makes Life Difficult,"
Pastor Rick's Daily Hope. May 21, 2014. Accessed
March 21, 2018. http://pastorrick.com/
devotional/english/rebellion-makes-life-difficult.

48. Alison Hsiao, "Teen pregnancies threaten mother
and child: bureau," *Taipei Times.* July 14, 2013.
Accessed on March 19, 2018. http://www.taipei
times.com/News/taiwan/archives/2013/07/14/
2003567082.

49. "Teen Pregnancy Statistics," *TeenHelp.* Accessed
March 20, 2018. https://www.teenhelp.com/teen-
pregnancy/teen-pregnancy-statistics/.

50. "Abortion Laws Worldwide," *Women on Waves.*
Accessed March 18, 2018. http://www.women
onwaves.org/en/page/460/abortion-laws-
worldwide.

51. "Welcome to our Testimony Directory," *Silent No
More Awareness.* Accessed March 17, 2018. http://
www.silentnomoreawareness.org/testimonies/.

52. Ibid.

53. Friedrich Nietzsche, *The Gay Science* (1882, 1887)
para. 125; Walter Kaufmann ed. (New York:
Vintage, 1974), 181-182.

54. Abraham Lincoln, AZ Quotes. Accessed March 21,
2018. http://www.azquotes.com/quote/392145.

55. Nick Gillespie, "Millennials Are Selfish and
Entitled, and Helicopter Parents Are to Blame,"
Time. August 21, 2014. Accessed on March 11,

2018. http://time.com/3154186/millennials-selfish-entitled-helicopter-parenting/.

56. David Foster Wallace, *The Pale King* (New York: Back Bay Books, 2011), 138.

57. The quotation has been simplified from an interview with journalist Llew Gardner for Thames Television's *This Week* program on February 5, 1976 (https://www.snopes.com/fact-check/other-peoples-money/).

58. For a good read on this subject, see http://www.inquiriesjournal.com/articles/362/you-owe-me-examining-a-generation-of-entitlement.

59. Thomas A. Garrett, "100 Years of Bankruptcy: Why More Americans Than Ever Are Filing," *Federal Reserve Bank of St. Louis.* Spring 2006. Accessed March 18, 2018. https://www.stlouisfed.org/publications/bridges/spring-2006/100-years-of-bankruptcy-why-more-americans-than-ever-are-filing.

60. "Household debt in Asia," *The Economist.* November 2, 2013. Accessed on March 19, 2018. https://www.economist.com/news/economic-and-financial-indicators/21588882-house hold-debt-asia.

61. Ibid.

62. University of Minnesota, "Involving Children in Household Tasks: Is It Worth the Effort?" September 2002. Accessed March 12, 2018. http://ghk.h-cdn.co/assets/cm/15/12/55071e0298a05_-_Involving-children-in-household-tasks-U-of-M.pdf.

63. From Tolkien's *Lord of the Rings* trilogy, "Precious" is the name of the ring of power which slowly perverted and controlled whoever possessed it. Mordor is the region where the ring was forged, and the only place where it could be destroyed.

64. G. K. Chesterton, "G. K. Chesterton: Quotes: Quotable Quotes," *Goodreads*. Accessed March 11, 2018. https://www.goodreads.com/quotes/73243-there-are-two-ways-to-get-enough-one-is-to.

65. "Give a Man a Fish, and You Feed Him for a Day," *Quote Investigator*. Accessed on March 21, 2018. https://quoteinvestigator.com/2015/08/ 28/fish/.

66. Larry Winget, "How To Take Responsibility," *Larry Winget, The Pitbull of Personal Responsibility*®. Accessed March 21, 2018. http://www.larry winget.com/how-to-take-responsibility/.

67. Kay Wills Wyma, "Cleaning House Quotes," *Goodreads*. Accessed on March 19, 2018. https://www.goodreads.com/work/quotes/18325918-cleaning-house-a-mom-s-twelve-month-experiment-to-rid-her-home-of-youth.

68. "Feeding a 'Why Work Mindset?'" *Newstral*. August 6, 2015. Accessed March 20, 2018. https://newstral.com/en/article/en/997466691/feeding-a-why-work-mindset-most-states-waiving-food-stamp-work-regs-raising-gov-t-dependency-worry.

69. Abraham Lincoln, AZ Quotes. Accessed March 21, 2018. http://www.azquotes.com/quote/392145.

70. Dava Sobel, "Work Habits in Childhood Found to

Predict Adult Well-Being," *The New York Times*. November 10, 1981. Accessed on March 12, 2018. https://www.nytimes.com/1981/11/10/science/work-habits-in-childhood-found-to-predict-adult-well-being.html.

71. Ibid.

72. Pablo Diaz, "The Healing Power of Forgiveness," Guideposts. Accessed on March 21, 2018. https://www.guideposts.org/better-living/positive-living/the-healing-power-of-forgiveness.

73. Matthew 18:7 (NKJV).

74. Chris Thomas, *Wishing for the Day* (Anchored Hope Ministries, 2009), 39.

75. Marianne Williamson, "Beliefnet's Inspirational Quotes," *Beliefnet*. Accessed March 20, 2018. http://www.beliefnet.com/quotes/relationships/n/no-title/the-practice-of-forgiveness.aspx.

76. "Forgiveness: Your Health Depends on It," *John Hopkins Medicine*. Accessed on March 21, 2018. https://www.hopkinsmedicine.org/health/healthy_aging/healthy_connections/forgiveness-your-health-depends-on-it.

77. Ibid.

78. Ibid.

79. John Bunyan, *Pilgrim's Progress*. (Chicago: Moody Publishers, 2007), 51-52.

80. Matthew 18:22 (NKJV).

ABOUT THE AUTHOR

(L to R) Anthony, Liz, Maisha, Nate, Daniel, Anna, Charlotte, Tabitha, Jeremy, Joyce, and Kevin

Do Re Mi Fa So La Ti . . . *The Sound of Music* is one of the most watched movies ever. Who could forget the joyous image of a family of seven children riding bikes through the town, singing songs, and spreading cheer at every turn. Kevin has often felt like this is exactly what his family is like. They've been blessed so that they can be a blessing, and whether or not they are singing, their joy is contagious.

When the famed von Trapp family fled their native Austria at the end of the film, they settled just a short distance from Kevin's family homestead in the Green Mountains of Vermont, where Graves family has been since the 1760s! In fact, members of Kevin's family are friends with several of the von Trapps.

Kevin's sense of adventure was birthed in these mountains as well, where he reveled in his love for the outdoors: hunting, fishing, hiking, camping, snowshoeing and skiing, just to name a few. He carried this same adventurous spirit with him to Asia at the age of twenty-three, where his love of the peoples and cultures caused him

Cynthia and Nathan

naturally to fall in love with Joyce. Married in Hong Kong 1985, they started a family, and before you know it—Do Re Mi—we had seven of our own as well. Add to this two sons-in-law, a daughter-in-law, and two grandchildren, and we have the makings of a choir! Our children, aged ten to thirty, have also caught the same sense of adventure. One time, he mused that they were spread out in five nations and three continents at the same time! So if you happen to see a large family coming down the street and singing one day, stop and say, "Hello."

Sylvia

Joyce and Kevin, and sometimes some of their kids, also do a lot of traveling around Asia (and occasionally in North America) speaking about families. Whether on the street, or at a conference, or back in Vermont at the Trapp Family Lodge (where the family picture was taken), we hope to high five you some day, and spread just a little bit more cheer.

For more information or to contact Kevin, email him at Info.ilikemyparents@gmail.com.

44673890R00144

Made in the USA
Middletown, DE
13 May 2019